Know Thyself

D0145336

Know Thyself: The Value and Limits of Self-Knowledge takes the reader on a tour of the nature, value, and limits of self-knowledge. Mitchell S. Green calls on classical sources like Plato and Descartes, twentieth-century thinkers like Freud, recent developments in neuroscience and experimental psychology, and even Buddhist philosophy to explore topics at the heart of who we are. The result is an unvarnished look at both the achievements and drawbacks of the many attempts to better know one's own self.

Key topics in this volume include:

- Knowledge—what it means to know, the link between wisdom and knowledge, and the value of living an "examined life";
- Personal identity—questions of dualism (the idea that our mind is not *only* our brain), bodily continuity, and personhood;
- The unconscious—including the kind posited by psychoanalysis as well as the form proposed by recent research on the so-called adaptive unconscious;
- Free will—if we have it, and the recent arguments from neuroscience challenging it;
- Self-misleading—the ways we willfully deceive ourselves, and how this relates to empathy, peer disagreement, implicit bias, and intellectual humility;
- Experimental psychology—considerations on the automaticity of emotion and other cognitive processes, and how they shape us.

This book is designed to be used in conjunction with the free Know Thyself MOOC (massive open online course) created through collaboration of the University of Connecticut's Project on Humility and Conviction in Public Life, and the University of Edinburgh's Eidyn research centre, and hosted on the Coursera platform (https://www.coursera.org/learn/know-thyself). The book is also suitable as a text for interdisciplinary courses in the philosophy of mind or self-knowledge, and is highly recommended for anyone looking for a short overview of this fascinating topic.

Mitchell S. Green received a B.A. from the University of California, Berkeley, a B.Phil. from the University of Oxford, and a Ph.D. from the University of Pittsburgh. He currently teaches at the University of Connecticut. In addition to approximately 50 journal articles and book chapters, he has also published *Self-Expression, Engaging Philosophy: A Brief Introduction*, and *Moore's Paradox: New Essays on Belief, Rationality and the First Person* (co-edited with J. Williams).

Know Thyself

The Value and Limits
of Self-Knowledge

Mitchell S. Green

Routledge
Taylor & Francis Group

NEW YORK AND LONDON

Know Thyself
Free Online Course

This completely free and online course is designed to be used in conjunction with *Know Thyself: On the Value and Limits of Self-Knowledge*. Each week the book's author talks you through some of the central issues relating to self-knowledge including the unconscious, the value of the "examined life", wisdom, the varieties of knowledge, empathy, the nature of the self, and even challenges to the existence of a self. No prior knowledge of philosophy is required. Students who successfully complete the course are eligible for a certificate of completion from Coursera.

The Massive Open Online Course (MOOC) has been created through collaboration between the University of Connecticut's Humility and Conviction in Public Life project, and the University of Edinburgh's Eidyn research centre, and is offered by Coursera.

Watch introductory video
and sign up for the course at:
www.coursera.org/learn/know-thyself

Taught by Dr. Mitchell S. Green

First published 2018
by Routledge
711 Third Avenue, New York, NY 10017

and by Routledge
2 Park Square, Milton Park, Abingdon, Oxon, OX14 4RN

Routledge is an imprint of the Taylor & Francis Group, an informa business

Library of Congress Cataloging-in-Publication Data
Names: Green, Mitchell S., author.Title: Know thyself : on the value
    and limits of self-knowledge / Mitchell S. Green.
Description: New York : Routledge, [2018] | Includes bibliographical
    references and index.
Identifiers: LCCN 2017028452 | ISBN 9781138675995 (hbk) |
    ISBN 9781138676022 (pbk) | ISBN 9781315560298 (ebk)
Subjects: LCSH: Self (Philosophy) | Self-knowledge, Theory of.
Classification: LCC BD438.5 .G74 2018 | DDC 126—dc23
LC record available at https://lccn.loc.gov/2017028452

ISBN: 978-1-138-67599-5 (hbk)
ISBN: 978-1-138-67602-2 (pbk)
ISBN: 978-1-315-56029-8 (ebk)

Typeset in Times New Roman
by Apex CoVantage, LLC

In memory of my father, Burton Green,
teacher and student

Contents

Preface

It is an oft-repeated precept that we should know ourselves. Yet it is not clear what kind of knowledge this advice is telling us to acquire, or how to acquire it. We hear a lot of advice, not all of which, on closer examination, is particularly plausible. Might the injunction to achieve self-knowledge be over-rated, one of those old pieties that we do better to leave behind? After all, there are many interesting things to know. Why should knowing ourselves be singled out from among these as in any way special? And even if self-knowledge is important or special, doesn't each of us know enough about ourselves already? Like you, I know when I am hungry, or cold, or want to go see a movie. So what is the problem?

In this book I hope to make some progress in answering these questions. In particular I will first elucidate the phenomenon—or better, phenomena—of self-knowledge, and some of the complexity that confronts us when we attempt to come to terms with it. On that basis I will offer an explanation of why striving for self-knowledge is of value, while also keeping in view the barriers to which our attempts to know ourselves are prone. This explanation will not be able to address all possible forms of skepticism: there will likely be some readers left who remain unpersuaded. That is quite okay. I do hope that even such skeptics will be able to appreciate the reasons why someone might take a different approach from theirs. Further, I hope you will find some intrinsic interest in engaging with the ides of some great thinkers of the past, as well as with some major current issues in ongoing debates about the self and our knowledge of it.

I have written this book with the conviction that virtually anyone with some curiosity about and interest in living a good life might be interested in the topic of self-knowledge: its nature, its value, and also its limits. However, I shall do my best to earn your agreement rather than take it for granted. In so doing I have not presupposed any background knowledge other than the general information about the world that most of us have by about the time we are teenagers. I have also assumed that the reader is able to follow a line of reasoning and think about some abstract concepts, but I have tried to exhibit such lines of reasoning and present those abstract ideas relatively gently. As is characteristic of my field of philosophy, my main aim is not to provide advice or definitive answers as to how to achieve self-knowledge or attain the kind of life that it might help promote. Some pointers toward self-knowledge will of course emerge in our discussion, for instance when we look into the topics of self-deception and what I call self-misleading. Nonetheless, my main aim is to provide the reader with some tools for making headway on her own, or with friends, peers, or family members, in discussing, thinking through, and learning more about these topics. While I will be showing you around the territory that is self-knowledge—its promontories, valleys, dangerous areas, and curiosities—my main aim is to convey the skills you might find useful in navigating it well after you complete this book.

Academic philosophy in the last two centuries, at least in Western countries, has tended to promote an image of the field as one that is studied in solitude: we are familiar with the image of the professor or student reading or writing in private as she contemplates an ancient problem of mind, matter, ethics, or knowledge. Rodin's sculpture, *The Thinker* (*La Penseur*), well captures this sensibility.

This image is, however, at odds with philosophy's ancient origins, whether they be that of the Buddha discussing hard questions in the Himalayan foothills with his disciples, or Socrates debating with acquaintances in the marketplace in Athens. It is also at odds with what I believe to be the most fruitful and enjoyable way to engage with the field: you will probably learn more, and have more fun in the process, engaging with philosophy in the company of others whether you do so in a traditional college class, an in-person or virtual discussion group, or the massive open online course (MOOC) with which the book shares a name. In that spirit I have attempted to write this book in such a way as to give the reader a sense of participating in a conversation, not only with me but with some of the thinkers that I discuss. Here too I hope to incite further conversation rather than end dialogue with any final statements.

I have also written this book in such a way as to make it to conducive to classroom use. Each chapter ends with a bulleted overview of the main points, as well as study questions which could be used as prompts for class discussion, examination questions, and paper topics. I have also listed introductory and more advanced further readings for those students interested in exploring a topic in greater depth. In addition, and in light of my experience teaching courses on self-knowledge for about 10 years, each of the first four chapters of this book is associated with one primary text that would be suitable for use in parallel with this one. The associations are as follows:

1.	Socrates and the Examined Life	Plato, *Five Dialogues*
2.	Descartes' Essence	Descartes, *Meditations on First Philosophy*
3.	Ryle's Re-Casting of the "Mind-Body Problem"	Ryle, *The Concept of Mind*
4.	The Freudian Unconscious	Freud, *Introductory Lectures on Psychoanalysis*

In addition, for those offering courses of potential interest to students in the cognitive sciences outside of philosophy (particularly psychology, neuroscience, computer science, or linguistics), Chapter 5 (on the "adaptive unconscious") is well paired with T. Wilson's *Strangers to Ourselves*, and with A. Damasio's *Descartes' Error*. Finally, Siderits' *Buddhism as Philosophy* is exceptionally well suited to complement the final two chapters of this book. (Full citations are found at the end of the relevant chapters, as well as in the comprehensive bibliography.) Those familiar with the main current of contemporary philosophical literature on self-knowledge will recognize that this volume is out of the mainstream: our focus is only passingly on such questions as how we know our current mental states, such as one's belief that the sun is shining outside. Instead, the book is written in the same spirit as that of Cassam, who focuses on what he terms substantial self-knowledge.[1]

Thanks are due to many who helped me in bringing this project into being. First to Andy Beck of Routledge who initially suggested that I write the volume; my thanks to him for his guidance and serene patience. I am grateful also to Vera Lochtefeld of Routledge whose good sense and attention to detail saved me from numerous errors. Emma Bjorngard has been a research assistant nonpareil, with astute comments on chapter drafts and useful ideas for illustrative examples. Olta Shkembi painstakingly read the entire manuscript and offered myriad insightful comments along the way. I am also grateful to the Center for Contemplative Mind in Society, whose course development grant in 2005 enabled me to spend uninterrupted time developing the course that initially inspired this book. Likewise, the Honors Program at the University of Connecticut provided me with further course development support, as well as a steady supply of outstanding students on whom I have been able to test out preliminary chapters.

Finally, my thanks to Lori, Noah, Sofia, and Clementine for being the best family I could imagine having, providing love, emotional support, comic relief, and tolerance for my obsessiveness. Clementine's and my collective six legs have walked thousands of miles while we reflected on the self and our knowledge of it. If Plato's argument in *Republic* that dogs are lovers of wisdom (because they are kind toward those they know, and fierce toward those they don't know) is cogent, then she is the ultimate peripatetic philosopher.

Note

1. Q. Cassam (2014) *Self-Knowledge for Humans* (Oxford: Oxford University Press). Unlike Cassam, I see no reason to restrict the subject to our own species.

1   Socrates and the Examined Life

Introduction

We begin our exploration of self-knowledge in Athens of 399 BC, where Socrates is defending himself against serious accusations that have been brought against him by some fellow Athenians. Among the many points he makes in his own defense is that his friend Chaerephon has consulted the Oracle at Delphi, who told him that no one is wiser than Socrates. Socrates had long professed ignorance about life's most important matters, so he is perplexed by the Oracle's pronouncement. However, he suggests that perhaps he is at least cognizant of his own ignorance while many of his fellow Athenians are not. We will explore this suggestion and relate it to Socrates' later remark that the unexamined life is not worth living. Although many of us have heard this claim so often as to be nearly complacent about it, it is controversial. As a result, we will consider reasons for thinking the remark unreasonably demanding. We will also consider a reinterpretation of Socrates' dictum making it both more plausible and more interesting than its more typical construal. In light of this reinterpretation, we will be able to discern ways in which people can live lives that would likely be richer and more rewarding if they were to find room for self-examination. Finally, characters from other Platonic dialogues (including Ion, Crito, Glaucon, and Euthyphro), as well as some familiar slogans from contemporary life, are discussed in order to illustrate various failures of self-examination.

A Puzzling Oracle

The phrase "Know thyself" is an English translation of the Greek dictum,

ΓΝΩΘΙ ΣΑΥΤΟΝ

These words were, according to legend, carved into stone at the entrance to the temple of Apollo at Delphi, Greece. This temple dates at least as far back as the eighth century BC, and was at the height of its influence between the sixth and fourth centuries BC. The dictum is only one of over 100 that were visible in various parts of the temple. Among the others were "Shun murder," "Crown your ancestors," and "Control the eye." However, the injunction to know oneself is probably the most famous of all of them. This is partly due to the association of this phrase with Socrates and his student Plato. To understand this association, it helps to appreciate the role of the Temple at Delphi in Greek life in the fourth century BC. According to Greek legend, Zeus released two eagles at opposite ends of the world, and they met at what is now Delphi, which as a result came to be called *omphalos* or the navel of the world. According to one archeological study, on the site of the temple an intoxicating vapor flowed out of a subterranean cavern (Spiller et al. 2003). A priestess known as the Pythian would inhale this vapor and enter an altered state of consciousness through which she was believed to serve as the mouthpiece of a deity. As a result, it was thought that the priestess could not be in error in answering questions put to her. However, perhaps due to her intoxication, the Pythian's utterances required interpretation. Consequently, (male) priests would act as intermediaries between the Pythian and the public. But even with the aid of their interpretation, the priests' words had to be construed carefully. Leaders of city-states (or their emissaries) from all over greater Greece would come to Delphi seeking the Pythian's advice. One legend has it that King Croesus of Lydia consulted the oracle to determine whether he should attack Cyrus the Great and his Persian army. The oracle replied that if he attacked the Persians, he would destroy a great empire. Croesus took this reply as advice to attack, but when he did so, his army, and consequently his own empire, were destroyed.

Socrates (469 to 399 BC) was the son of a midwife and a sculptor, and he spent the great majority of his 70 years living in Athens. Most days he could be found in the agora, which in Athens served as marketplace, social venue, and locus of much politicking. Rather than work in a job such as sculpting or sandal-making, Socrates could usually be found here engaging in conversation with a respected Athenian citizen or one of the city's many visitors. In these conversations, Socrates would typically raise a question about the nature of justice, virtue, piety, or knowledge. More often than not, Socrates would show his interlocutors that their answers to his questions were unacceptable in some way, for instance as a result of being either inconsistent or not cohering with something else that they professed to believe.

This way of conducting himself had two consequences. First, it gained for Socrates a small band of followers who found these conversations fascinating. These followers were aristocratic young men who had the leisure to spend their days in discussion rather than at work. Among the young men in his entourage are Crito, Xenophon, Cratylus, and Plato, who came to write down many of the dialogues he witnessed between Socrates and others.

Second, Socrates' way of conducting himself, and the entourage of aristocratic followers it generated, over time provoked the ire of some of Athens' more prominent citizens. Some of them might have been parents of the aforementioned young men; others might have been among those whose conversations with Socrates showed that they knew less about virtue, wisdom, and the like than they thought they did. This ire grew over the years until a formal accusation was lodged against Socrates. According to this accusation, Socrates has been corrupting the youth of Athens; he does not believe in the gods accepted by society, and he "makes the better argument seem the worse," which apparently was a way of saying that he tends to confuse people with complicated lines of reasoning. Shortly after this, Socrates finds himself on trial in front of a jury of his peers. (In Athens at the time, such a jury would have consisted of 501 male, landholding Athenian citizens.) His aim is to defend himself against these charges in an effort to show that none of them is accurate. (Our primary source of information about this event is the description written down by Socrates' student Plato. This description is known as the "Apology," but do not be misled by this term, which is just a transliteration of the original Greek term. In defending himself, Socrates is not apologetic in the least. Instead, he aims to explain and justify his actions, and to show his fellow Athenians that he is innocent of the charges that have been leveled against him.)

As part of his self-defense, Socrates denies that he knows much of anything. To explain what he means by this, Socrates contrasts his own lifestyle with that of sophists, who travel from one polis, or city-state, to another charging a fee to anyone wishing to hear them profess on topics of interest. One such sophist is Evenus, whose fee is 500 drachmas (one drachma being about what a laborer earned in a day). Socrates tells his audience that he would be very proud of himself if he had the knowledge that Evenus professes to have. Unfortunately, however, he has no such knowledge. But then, in a move that may seem to contradict what he had just said, Socrates relates the tale of his old friend Chaerephon, who had gone to consult the oracle at Delphi. Chaerephon asked the oracle whether anyone is wiser then Socrates. The oracle replied that no, no one is wiser than Socrates!

How could Socrates be speaking the truth about his lack of knowledge if no one is wiser than he? Keeping in mind the legend about the trouble that came to Croesus from his hasty interpretation of the oracle's words, let's be careful about the oracle's answer to Chaerephon's question. If no one is wiser than Socrates, that might simply be because everyone is equally unwise. (So too, it may be that no one in the room is taller than Yael, not because she is taller than everyone else, but rather because everyone in the room, including Yael, is exactly the same height.) In spite of this, Socrates interprets the oracle's answer as indicating that he is wiser than others, if only by a slight margin. Further, Socrates tells his audience that he found the oracle's answer unbelievable. Surely someone out there must be wiser than he is! So, Socrates tells the jurors, after Chaerephon reported the oracle's answer, he set about trying to prove that the oracle was mistaken by finding someone wiser than he. However, after many years of talking to others from various walks of life (including poets, artisans, and politicians), Socrates concluded that all these people believe themselves to be wise, but are mistaken in that belief. For instance, Socrates went to the poets to ask them to explain their works. They were, however, unable to do so. As Socrates recalls, "Almost all the bystanders might have explained the poems better than their authors could" (*Five Dialogues*, p. 27). Similarly, artisans certainly know better than Socrates how to cut and shape wood to be used in the bow of a trireme, or how to fashion an urn. However, all too often such people take their skills to qualify them to pronounce on great questions of justice, virtue, and the like; and here Socrates found that their views on these matters are not well supported.

These experiences helped Socrates to see how the oracle might have been right after all. For while others lack wisdom but think themselves to be wise, Socrates acknowledges his own lack of wisdom. He appreciates his own limitations, whereas others are too self-confident or complacent, or both to even notice their own. Socrates narrates his conclusion as follows:

> So I withdrew and thought to myself: "I am wiser than this man; it is likely that neither of us knows anything worthwhile, but he thinks he knows something when he does not, whereas when I do not know, neither do I think I know; so I am likely to be wiser than he to this small extent, that I do not think I know what I do not know."
>
> (*Five Dialogues*, p. 26)

Socrates' conclusion seems to vindicate the oracle's pronouncement while still making sense of why he tells his jurors that he does not have knowledge that could be used to corrupt the youth of Athens. After all, if you know nothing, or nothing of importance, then merely being aware of this fact does not exactly qualify you to go around Greece charging people 500 drachmas to hear you speak!

We may see the idea behind the Oracle's pronouncement even more clearly once we note a distinction between knowledge and wisdom. To prepare for that distinction, first consider the concept of knowledge as the Western philosophical tradition has primarily understood it since the time of the Greeks. According to this tradition, what we know are propositions (such as that $2 + 2 = 4$, or that Windhoek is the capital of Namibia). This type of knowledge is thus known as *propositional knowledge* (It will be contrasted with another kind—ability knowledge—in Chapter 3.) Further, if we are to know a proposition it must, first of all, be true. (One cannot *know* that $2 + 2 = 5$; the most one can do is be, for whatever odd reason, certain that it is true.) Second, if we are to know a proposition, we must also believe it to be true. (One cannot know a proposition on which one is, say, entirely agnostic.) And finally, even if a proposition is true, and one believes that it is, that does not guarantee that one knows this proposition. To see why, suppose that the town in which I live is having a contest to see who can guess the number of marbles in a large jar sitting at the center of the town square. Without even going to inspect the jar, I mail in my guess: 43,297. Lo and behold, I was right! That is exactly the number of marbles in the jar, and as a result I win a pair of free airline tickets to Namibia. This is wonderful news, since that is a country I've wanted to visit since I was a teenager. However, in spite of being glad that I won the contest I do not think others should say that I knew how many marbles there are in the jar. A mere lucky guess is not sufficient for knowledge.

Matters would be different in this case had I gone to the town square with a tape measure and calculated as best I could the number of marbles in the jar on the basis of my measurements. Or even more dramatically, suppose I crept into the town square under the cover of darkness, emptied out the entire jar, counted each one of the marbles that fell out, and then refilled the jar's contents and crept away without being detected. Here it seems clear that if I had then sent in my answer (43,297) on the basis of that painstaking counting, I did know how many marbles were in that jar. Socrates in other dialogues would say that in order to have knowledge one must make not just a lucky guess, but also have an account, that is, some basis for the thing that you believe. Present-day philosophers would put the point by saying that knowledge requires not just truth and belief, but also *justification*: you must be able to give reasons for the things you take yourself to know. It is common nowadays to crystallize the result of this line of thought by referring to the "jtb" account of knowledge: propositional knowledge requires justified, true belief.[1]

With propositional knowledge roughly characterized, we may now see that one can be (propositionally) knowledgeable without being wise. One can, that is, absorb a great deal of information (and do so by reliable means in such a way to achieve justification) and still not make use of it in a way that benefits oneself or others. Someone with extensive knowledge of the causes and varieties of disease would hardly seem wise if she does not use this information to help keep herself or others from falling ill. Conversely, one who is not well-informed may still exhibit wisdom by acknowledging that fact. Otherwise he is liable to do something rash based on what he *thinks* he knows to be the case. King Croesus, for instance, *thought* he knew what the Delphic oracle meant in saying that if he attacked the Persians, a great empire would be destroyed. But he did not. Had he instead acknowledged that the oracle's answer could be construed either as a suggestion that he go to war or as a warning against doing so, he might have refrained from attacking the Persians and thereby saved his kingdom from destruction. So too, Socrates would seem after all to be wiser than his fellow Athenians: although all in the polis lack answers to life's important questions, Socrates alone acknowledges his ignorance and so is less likely than his compatriots are to do rash things presupposing such unjustified answers.

The Examined Life, Take 1

Although Socrates makes a vigorous case in reply to the charges that have been brought against him, the jury votes and finds him guilty as charged; what is more, after further discussion the jury sentences him to die by drinking the poisonous nectar of the hemlock plant. To the amazement of many modern readers, the record of the trial does not describe Socrates as terribly upset by this verdict. He does not attempt to plea for mercy from his fellow Athenians. Nor does he beg to be sent into exile in another city-state such as Thebes or Megara. His reason for refusing exile is not that he will be terribly distraught over missing his friends and family in Athens. Rather, his reason seems to be that to avoid being put on trial yet again in his new home, wherever that may be, he would have to keep his mouth shut rather than spending his days asking philosophical questions of whomever might be willing to listen. But, Socrates suggests, that would be no way to live. He sums up this line of thought with words commonly translated as the

Socratic Dictum:
The unexamined life is not worth living for men.

This turns out to be one of the more famous statements in the Western philosophical tradition. What does it mean, and is it true? The first thing to consider about this dictum is that it refers to the notion of an examined life. Modern readers might understand this idea of an examined life in terms of *introspection* into one or more of our psychological states. According to this modern approach, I engage in self-examination by focusing on my thoughts, emotions, or experiences and perhaps also attending to their features. Thus I might notice that the sour taste in my mouth is a bit less intense than it was a few minutes ago, or that the irritation I am feeling toward the airplane passenger in the seat behind me is gradually increasing. However, the ancient Greeks seem to have had a conception of an examined life in which introspection plays a marginal role at best. At least as Socrates understands the notion, living an examined life seems to involve spending time trying to understand fundamental concepts such as virtue, justice, knowledge, and piety. Further, because virtue, justice, knowledge, and piety must characterize any life that is lived well, self-examination would seem to be a necessary step to living a good life. But how does one understand such a thing as virtue? Socrates' answer is not that one does so by introspecting on one's concept of virtue (even supposing that such a thing were possible), but rather it is by engaging in debate with others about how best to define virtue. Is virtue something that can be learned, for instance; can a successful city-state be led by a leader who is not himself virtuous, and so on. Further, in taking every opportunity to discuss with others the nature of virtue (or justice, or knowledge, or any other central facet of a life well lived), we are also examining ourselves, for it is in debate on these topics that we are forced to elucidate, and often revise, our own views in response to the questions and challenges of others. By contrast, an unexamined life is one in which we do not engage in conversation with others or even ourselves about the nature of these fundamental concepts, but rather behave in accordance with our unreflective grasp of those concepts.

Another aspect of the Socratic Dictum is that, strictly speaking, it refers only to men. Ancient Greece was a profoundly sexist society, with women having a social status only slightly higher than that of slaves. As a result, it might not have occurred to Socrates or his jurors to ask whether the unexamined life is worth living for women. While acknowledging this disturbing shortcoming of the Socratic Dictum and the society in which it was espoused, we may now see that restricting it to one gender only is arbitrary at best. For our purposes, even if we interpret the Dictum as applying to all persons regardless of gender, we will still have good reasons for doubting its accuracy.

Why is that? Well, as we have seen from Socrates' understanding of the examined life, in spending his days going around the agora and elsewhere in Athens interrogating others about concepts that are fundamental to a life well lived, Socrates is living an examined life. (He may also be examining other people's lives by asking them questions about their own views, but that is compatible with his examining his own.) Accordingly, in claiming that the unexamined life is not worth living, Socrates is in effect telling his audience that his life would not be worth living if he were to spend the rest of his days keeping his mouth shut, neither questioning others about their views, nor trying out his own ideas on his conversational partners.

Even bearing firmly in mind Socrates' way of understanding an examined or unexamined life, should we really go so far as to agree that staying silent about these questions would make one's life not worth living? Come to think of it, could a life ever not be worth living? After all, many people will agree that all life has value. But having value, and being worth living, are different things. Consider that according to some ethicists, some lives might fall below what they term the "zero line" and thus not be worth living (Glover 2008). Imagine for instance a baby named Mia born with a congenital disease that causes her to be in relentless pain. Mia seems to be forever uncomfortable, crying constantly, and never seems to acknowledge the existence of others, including her parents. After numerous failed operations to correct her condition, Mia passes away at age six months. You may understand why someone might feel that this baby's life was not worth living even though she had value for the entirety of her brief life.

The idea of a life not being worth living seems, then, to make sense. However, it is a huge leap from this admission to the conclusion that an unexamined life in Socrates' sense of that notion is not worth living. Even if he were to spend the rest of his days not debating with others the nature of justice, virtue, and the like, Socrates could still enjoy the company of others, eat good food, listen to beautiful music, and enjoy watching horse races at the Piraeus, the port city serving Athens. This seems a very different case from Mia's brief life full of suffering.

Indeed, if we were to accept Socrates' dictum we would have to conclude that a vast number of people now or in the past live or have lived lives not worth living. Yet some people have what appears to be an unreflective sense of right and wrong that they are able to act on without having to engage in debate about the concepts being presupposed. Pallavi, for instance, has known since childhood that she wants to devote all her efforts to the protection of animals who have been abused, and she works tirelessly to finds homes for these creatures rather than having them euthanized in the "kill shelters" where they are temporarily housed. Abdul, by contrast, wants to do all he can to locate sources of unpolluted water for villagers in his native country, for it simply seems obvious to him that without clean water his compatriots will never be able to achieve a decent standard of living. Both Pallavi and Abdul, we may further imagine, work very hard, and have precious little time or energy left over at day's end for debating about the nature of justice, virtue, wisdom, or the like. But both of them do a great deal of good: Pallavi has saved the lives of hundreds of animals and brought happiness to those who have provided homes for them, and Abdul has enabled countless families to drink water without being in danger of falling ill. Saying that Pallavi and Abdul live lives that are not worth living seems not just implausible, but even elitist. Is Socrates just mistaken in claiming that the unexamined life is not worth living?

A Reinterpretation of Socrates

The philosopher Richard Kraut has taken up this question in his essay, "The Examined Life" (Kraut 2009). He agrees that as we have interpreted it, Socrates' dictum seems unrealistic: too many people whose lives seem eminently worth living do not engage in self-examination as Socrates understands that notion. On the other hand, Kraut suggests, the original Greek formulation of the dictum may be read in more than one way. In addition to the construal of the dictum we have so far assumed, the Greek phrasing may also be read as

> *Socratic Dictum, Revised*
> The unexamined life is not to be lived.

Just a little reflection reveals how this differs from the original Socratic Dictum. Some years ago I was listening to a late-night jazz radio station, and between tracks the DJ said, of the piece he had just played, "Man, if you don't dig that, you got a hole in your soul!" As I reflected on his words, I realized that he was implying that your life is missing something of value if you are unable to appreciate the music, or at least the *type* of music, he had just played. And regardless of your opinion about jazz, I suspect that you may well agree that a life lived with no music at all is missing something of value. That life may still be worth living, but it is incomplete. We may even imagine a

> *Musician's Dictum*
> The unmusical life is not to be lived.

According to the Musician's Dictum, one who lives her life without music is missing something important even if her life is still worth living in its absence. We may readily think of similar dicta about friendship, love, exercise, and good food. Similarly, according to *Socratic Dictum, Revised*, we may say that if Pallavi or Abdul refrain from self-examination in Socrates' understanding of that activity, they may still live lives that are worth living, but those lives are missing something of value. What is more, this seems independently plausible: Pallavi does great things, but if she has never reflected on the reason why it is important to save animals from being euthanized, we may feel there is something hollow, perhaps even dogmatic, in her way of thinking. So too, while it may seem obvious that providing safe drinking water for people is a worthwhile activity, if Abdul cannot say why doing so is worthwhile, he would seem to be missing something of value.

Richard Kraut has given us a key to making Socrates' pronouncement about the unexamined life more reasonable. If we use it in an effort to unlock Socrates' point of view, it enables us to grasp why he might prefer to accept his penalty of death rather than go into exile. At the time of his trial, Socrates is 70 years of age—quite an advanced age for his time. Imagine another person—call him Ravi—who instead of being a philosopher is a 70-year-old music aficionado who has been accused by some of his compatriots of caring too much about music. Powerful officials put Ravi on trial, and find him guilty as charged. He is given the choice between death, on the one hand, and living, on the other, but only on the condition that he never listen to or play music again. One can understand why Ravi might choose death over a music-free life for the time that remains to him. So too, now that we have given it a closer look, Socrates' choice to accept his penalty of death rather than go into exile does not seem so absurd.

A Pluralist Challenge

We have now seen a fairly extreme, as well as a more moderate formulation of the value of an examined life. On the extreme interpretation, one who does not engage in self-examination might as well never have been born, while on the more moderate formulation, a life without self-examination may be worth living but is still missing something of value that any complete life would contain. Might there be a basis for challenging even this more moderate point of view as expressed in Socratic Dictum, Revised? Once we remind ourselves how much variation there can be among people's preferences, we may begin to discern a source of skepticism about even the more moderate approach. For many of us live lives that are missing something of value, even though we might take issue with the suggestion that we are living lives that are not to be lived. Why is this? One reason is that, at least for those not living in extreme poverty or under repressive regimes, contemporary life presents us with so many possibilities of fulfillment that no one could pursue them all with enough consistency and commitment to achieve the value that all these sources have to offer. Although many of these activities would have been inconceivable in Socrates' time, just consider a few of the things that people find today to provide great value:

> International travel, photography, helping children with special needs, ballroom dancing, inventing energy-efficient technologies, yoga, rock climbing, training service animals to help those with special needs, friendship, romantic love, raising children, composing music, collecting vintage comic books.

This is a brief portion of a very long list. By any reasonable standard, even a full life could not achieve all the things on the entire list, assuming that such a list could be written down. As a result, no one should accuse a person who does not do everything on the list of living a life that is not to be lived.

A lesson we may draw from these observations is that living a life that is missing something of value should not be equated with living a life that is not to be lived. Simply because our time and resources are limited, all of us live lives that are missing something of value. It is only if, among the enormous list of worthwhile activities, some are of greater value than others, that we might have a chance of concluding that certain ways of living are to be avoided. It seems clear that Socrates would say that self-examination (in his sense of that term) is one of the things of greater value; I am confident he would say it is more important than travel or dancing, for instance. But should we believe him?

Consider Ella, who is happy spending her days surfing the legendary waves off the coast of Cape Town, South Africa. Ella is such a good surfer that she can make a living at it, and regularly wins large sums of prize money in competitions. Ella has no interest in self-examination, but she also has little interest in music, fine food, or anything else that gets in the way of her pursuing her passion for surfing. Imagine Socrates telling her that she is living a life that is not to be lived because she is failing to engage in self-examination. Ella might reply that she has everything she needs, thank you, so long as there are wind, waves, and sunshine. Further, if her health ever fails and she has to give up surfing, perhaps she will take up another pursuit instead. But that doesn't mean she should start worrying about that now. So long as her legs are strong and the waves are good, she'll keep searching for the next great barrel ride.

Ella is expressing a view that we might call *pluralist*. She does not say that self-examination is without value. However, she challenges us to explain why it has greater value than any of the many other things that one might spend one's time doing. Further, she might tell us, given that there are far too many things worth doing to do them all, no item on the list of things that are worth doing has the feature that, if someone fails to do that thing, then she lives a life that is not to be lived.

Socrates might reply to Ella as follows: although Ella might get very lucky and surf every day until her very last, chances are good that well before then she will need to find other ways of spending her time. Perhaps weather patterns will change, causing the waves to become too dangerous to surf, or maybe she will tear some cartilage in her knee and be unable to repair the damage with surgery. Engaging in Socratic self-examination can serve as a kind of insurance against such events. It won't prevent such unfortunate events from occurring, but it will help Ella negotiate them with a minimum of trauma. For if she can start thinking sooner rather than later about what it is about surfing she likes so much (the exercise? the scenery? the sense of adventure? etc.), that can help her decide what to do with herself if she is ever forced to pursue something else.

More generally, we may see that the pluralist about what makes life valuable will reject both the Socratic Dictum as well as its weaker alternative, Socratic Dictum, Revised. However, we have also argued on Socrates' behalf that the pluralist is choosing not to insure herself against the dangers that all too often confront us: accidents, failing health, environmental change, and the like can all make it harder to do the things we love. Rather than just giving up on life after such upsetting events, one who has engaged in Socratic self-examination stands a good chance of knowing how to proceed from there in a way that will still enable her to live life in a way she finds satisfying.

Some Unexamined Lives

As the example of Ella the surfer suggests, perhaps not all ways of refraining from self-examination result in lives that are not to be lived. However, we do not have to search too far before encountering unreflective ways of living that do seem to merit criticism. We mentioned that among Socrates' entourage was Plato, who wrote descriptions of many of the conversations that Socrates had with others in Athens. After Socrates' death, Plato continued to write dialogues in which Socrates is discussing philosophical issues with others. However, the consensus among scholars today is that many of the dialogues written after Socrates' death were primarily fictional rather than based on discussions that Plato witnessed; furthermore, these dialogues were often opportunities for Plato to develop his own answers to philosophical questions. Fortunately, our purposes here do not require us to sort out which of the things Plato wrote were based on conversations that took place and which were fictional. For even if some of the characters Plato describes are fictional, we may still learn from them. For instance, another of the dialogues Plato wrote is entitled *Ion*, named after a man who was a rhapsode. Rhapsodes traveled around ancient Greece reciting stories from Homer, and were much sought after. However, Plato makes clear that although Ion has memorized a great deal of Homeric poetry, he understands little of the stories he is telling: he thus has no appreciation of the way in which such stories offer insight into human character, mortality, love, and the horrors of war. This suggests that although he might be making a living as a rhapsode, Ion would seem to be missing out on other things of value.

A second example is provided by Euthyphro, after whom another of Plato's dialogues has been named. Socrates bumps into him at the law courts and asks him what brings him there. Euthyphro replies that he has come there to prosecute his father for murder. Surprised, Socrates asks Euthyphro to explain why he would do such a thing, and Euthyphro replies that his father had been responsible for the death of one of the workers he employs. Socrates replies that only someone who is sure of the rightness of his actions would prosecute his own father, to which Euthyphro replies that he is indeed sure that he is doing the right thing. In particular, Euthyphro tells Socrates that he is sure that he is doing the *pious* thing in prosecuting his father in the present circumstance, and Socrates responds by asking him to explain just what piety is. In reply, Euthyphro holds that piety is doing what the gods approve of. (Remember that Greek society is polytheistic at this time.) Socrates replies by showing that this is at best a superficial understanding of piety. For surely, the fact that a god approves an action cannot be enough to make that action right. (The Greek gods were notoriously capable of doing terrible things.) Instead, rightness or wrongness must be due to something about the action itself, such as that it tends to bring about suffering, or that it is a gracious response to another's impoliteness. Socrates asks Euthyphro how he would reply to this question, but rather than making an effort to do so, Euthyphro brusquely tells him that he has another engagement and hurries away.

Here is a dramatic case in which a person not only seems to be missing something by failing to think more deeply about the nature of piety; even worse than that, Euthyphro seems to be willing to put his father's and indeed his entire family's well-being in jeopardy in light of his assumptions about what being pious requires. Of course, Euthyphro may well be doing the right thing in prosecuting his father, but his basis for doing so is dogmatic rather than reasoned. As a result, his choice is at best risky and at worst quite rash.

Another example is Plato's older brother Glaucon, who plays an important role in the long dialogue known as the *Republic*. At an early stage in the discussion described in this dialogue, interlocutors consider the story of the Ring of Gyges. This ring enables its owner to become invisible, thereby granting him considerable new powers. In the twenty-first century, with security technology being what it is, even invisibility would not give you access to everything you might wish to manipulate, such as your bank account information or your standardized test scores. However, one could easily imagine using the ring to sneak into, say, a jewelry store to liberate a few diamond earrings or luxury watches. Glaucon, considering the temptation that the Ring of Gyges would pose for him, asks Socrates why he should "do the right thing" and not use it for illicit purposes. Socrates' reply is too complicated to reproduce here in full. However, according to one simplified version of that reply, Glaucon's temptation to use the Ring of Gyges shows that if he were to gain power or wealth by illicit means, these things would be of little value to him. Most likely no amount of power or wealth would satisfy him, and in no case could he look at his possessions or power and take pride in a job well done. The very fact that Glaucon is tempted to use the Ring of Gyges, Socrates might suggest, shows that he is failing to live an adequately examined life.

For a fourth example, consider a character who appears in a dialogue named after him, Crito. In the narrative of this dialogue, Crito pays a visit to Socrates in his prison cell early in the morning of the day in which he is to be executed. Crito points out that he has enough money to bribe the jailer so that Socrates can escape before the time of his execution. He could work up a disguise for Socrates and get him away from danger without too much trouble. What's more, Crito points out, if he doesn't help Socrates escape, others will think badly of him for not helping him to do so. Maybe he was too cheap to bribe the jailer, they'll say, so let's hurry!

Socrates replies that Crito should be less worried about what others think of him, and more concerned about doing the right thing. Socrates goes on to argue that trying to escape prison at this point would be immoral. Here again, Socrates gives an argument for his position that has engaged and provoked countless scholars and other readers of this dialogue. But for our purposes, the crucial thing is that Socrates is in effect accusing Crito of living an insufficiently examined life. For relying on other people's judgment to determine what he should do presupposes that he cannot think for himself to figure that out. Further, given how often the opinion of the crowd is in error, Crito should at least make an effort to think for himself rather than let his choices be determined by what others will or might think of him.

It would be natural to feel at this point that even if the above characters—Euthyphro, Ion, Glaucon, and Crito—are not fictional but were historical individuals, still, they lived a very long time ago. Surely human society has progressed since then? I will remain neutral on the question whether the passage of time has made for an overall improvement, although the current popularity of Elvis impersonators might make one wonder whether Ion's approach has really died away. In any case, I urge you to consider the extent to which you, or someone you know personally, is living a life that could benefit from examination in Socrates' sense of that term. To see why it might be possible to benefit in this way, observe that we regularly hear slogans, some of which are repeated so often that they come to take on the appearance of self-evident platitudes. Here are a few that I've heard:

"If It Makes You Happy, It Can't Be That Bad"

This is a line from a Sheryl Crow song titled "If It Makes You Happy." Regardless of what we think of the song's musical strengths, we might have our doubts about the line. All else being equal, it seems perfectly acceptable to do things that make one happy. But imagine a man named Earl who is happy only when he is making others suffer, either psychologically by making them embarrassed or humiliated, or physically by causing them genuine pain. I assume that most of us would find Earl quite repulsive and would probably consider him a sadist. But if we accept Sheryl Crow's position, we would have to agree that what Earl is doing "can't be that bad" when he makes others suffer since it makes him happy. Closer examination of this dictum and its implications, would, I suggest, make us want at the very least to qualify it in some way.

"My Country, Right or Wrong!"

You may have attended a political rally or been involved in a movement via social media. Either way, it is quite possible you have heard this attitude expressed as a way of urging that commitment to one's country transcends any moral requirements. However, careful reflection on this position will lead many people to recoil from it. What if your country is engaging in discrimination against a racial minority, or for that matter genocide against part of its population? Would you still follow your country's policy and defend it against all challengers?

Some people would answer this question in the affirmative. Others might find, in light of the scenarios just raised, that commitment to one's country has limits; beyond those limits, civil disobedience may be justified and perhaps even morally required.

"Everything Happens for a Reason"

I have heard this slogan countless times. In everyday contexts it is not said as an affirmation of universal causality, which would contradict accepted principles of quantum mechanics. Rather, it is normally said as a way of suggesting that when something befalls a person, such as life-threatening illness or failure to get the job of her dreams, that person will still gain something from the experience. From the life-threatening illness, she might acquire a new appreciation of the days that she still has remaining to her; from the failure to get the job, perhaps she will learn that she is not as qualified as she thought she was, or she may pursue an alternate career that to her surprise she finds extremely satisfying.

While it is always comforting to hear of people who triumph over, or at least are not entirely defeated by adversity, only a little examination of the present dictum will show that it is too strong. We easily forget those many occasions on which something bad happens and no one benefits as a result. Accordingly, someone striving to live an examined life will look at a slogan like this one and conclude that while it expresses a superficially reasonable attitude, on closer examination it turns out to be not terribly plausible.

"Better Safe Than Sorry"

You may have heard this advice from someone warning you not take a course of action you're considering that may carry some risks. Sometimes traveling in dangerous weather, or lending money to a friend, are more risky than their potential benefits would justify. However, if you examine the dictum a bit more carefully, you might begin to wonder how valuable a guide to action it really is. It is no doubt better to be safe than sorry; but if this dictum is used to justify not taking any risks, then surely our reasoning has gone wrong somewhere. Nearly everything we do involves *some* element of risk. Whether a given course of action is worth taking depends not just on whether it involves some risk, but also on whether its potential benefits—and costs if things don't go well—are great enough to make taking the risk worthwhile. Imagine someone uttering, "Better safe than sorry!" as a reason for never traveling on a plane, or for that matter not going on a blind date. These policies would be questionable at best. The difficulty, then, with saying it is better to be safe than sorry, is that in a given case of action being considered, this platitude won't tell us whether the risk is worth taking—and sometimes risks *are* worth taking.

In this chapter we have considered a notion of self-examination from ancient times and weighed its merits. I hope to have made it at least plausible that Socrates' understanding of self-examination has value, and that this value is not just in its ability to help us appreciate the failings of people who lived over two millennia ago. Instead, Socratic self-examination has worth even now as a way of helping us to consider some of the principles on which we act and to ask whether those principles are really viable. All too often, I suggest, we may find that those principles are in need of refinement, and in some cases they deserve to be rejected outright. The best way to learn more about Socratic self-examination is to try it out, preferably in the company of others patient enough to reflect on your questions about some of our basic assumptions concerning how to live.

Is this a task that could ever end? That is, have we reason to hope that with the help of enough patient and insightful interlocutors, we could finally reach agreement on the nature of justice, virtue, piety, and like notions? Some people will say that on such matters there are no right answers. However, there are two reasons to suspect that this attitude may be rash. First of all, we may ask how one could possibly know that there are no right answers to questions like these. Have you considered all possible answers and determined that none of them quite works? This seems very unlikely; if you had met as many creative, hardworking and insightful scholars as I have been fortunate enough to know, you might come to share my hope that one of them will write a dissertation, book, or journal article that is the definitive account of one of the concepts that Socrates and his friends puzzled over. Second, even if we remain neutral on the question whether it is possible to find definitive answers to these core philosophical concepts, we do know that progress has been and continues to be made. Contemporary theories of justice, for instance, are vastly more detailed, subtle, and powerful than those that were available to the ancients. Even if there are no absolutely definite answers, we seem to be making progress, so let's keep talking!

Finally, recall that we distinguished Socratic self-examination from the process of introspecting on one's own psychological states. We did not consider the merits or limitations of the latter approach, which has in fact been a dominant part of the Western philosophical tradition for approximately four centuries. In the next chapter we will begin to explore that tradition by considering the work of the philosopher widely considered the founder of what is known as the "modern" period of Western philosophy.

Chapter Summary

- The temple at ancient Delphi exhorted those visiting it to know themselves. This provides our first example of a people appealing to, and apparently placing value on, self-knowledge.
- Knowing oneself requires self-examination, but not in a sense that would come most naturally to contemporary readers. Instead, self-examination as understood by Socrates requires investigating, through debate and dialogue, the contours of concepts that seem necessary for living a good life: knowledge, justice, virtue, piety, and the like.
- Socrates heard that the oracle at Delphi had pronounced that no one was wiser than he. Socrates found this unbelievable and sought to disprove it. His years-long attempts to do so failed.

- Socrates learns from this failure that unlike those who mistakenly and complacently think themselves knowledgeable, he at least is aware of his shortcomings.
- Socrates is put on trial for a number of charges, and defends his actions by explaining that he was trying to disprove the oracle. He nevertheless is found guilty and sentenced to death.
- After his sentence, Socrates tells his audience that the unexamined life is not worth living. We may interpret this as implying that most people live lives that are not worth living; or we may take it to mean that the unexamined life is not to be lived. The latter seems a more reasonable interpretation of Socrates, though it is still challenged by a pluralist approach.
- Various characters from Plato's dialogues may be seen as failing to live examined lives. Even contemporary slogans suggest a lack of examination, since they must at least be qualified if they are to have a chance of plausibility.

Study Questions

1. What were the charges that were leveled against Socrates and on which he stood trial?
2. Does the statement "No one is wiser than Socrates" imply that Socrates is wiser than all others? Please explain your answer.
3. Why does Socrates appear to be uninterested in going into exile rather than accepting his death sentence?
4. How does the ancient Greek conception of self-examination differ from the contemporary concept of introspection?
5. Is it possible to be knowledgeable without being wise? Please explain your answer. Is it possible to be wise without being knowledgeable? Please explain your answer.
6. Please explain why the slogan "The unexamined life is not worth living" permits two readings, one of which seems more plausible than the other.
7. Please explain how the pluralist about the examined life would criticize the Socratic Dictum, Revised. Could the proponent of this revised dictum reply by drawing a comparison with the notion of insurance? Please explain your answer.
8. Can you think of any slogans you have heard (other than those mentioned above) that could benefit from further examination, refinement, or clarification? Please explain your answer.

Note

1. Since the early 1960s, controversy has raged over the question whether justified, true belief is *sufficient* for knowledge. Examples have emerged in which a person has justified, true belief and yet still does not seem to know the proposition that she believes. For further discussion see Pritchard (2009) and Pritchard (2014).

Introductory Further Reading

Glover, J. (2008) *Choosing Children: Genes, Disability, and Design* (Oxford: Oxford University Press). Accessible introduction to bioethics, including explanation of the concept of the "zero line."

Johnson, P. (2011) *Socrates: A Man for Our Times* (London: Viking). Accessible and well-written biography of Socrates.

Kitto, H.D.F. (1951) *The Greeks* (London: Penguin). Classic and highly readable general introduction to the world of ancient Greece.

Kraut, R. (2009) 'The Examined Life,' in S. Ahbel-Rapp and R. Kamtakar (eds.) *A Companion to Socrates* (Hoboken, NJ: Wiley-Blackwell), pp. 228–42. Argues for a more modest reading of the Socratic Dictum than is normally invoked.

Nails, D. (2009) 'The Trial and Death of Socrates,' in S. Ahbel-Rapp and R. Kamtakar (eds.) *A Companion to Socrates* (Hoboken, NJ: Wiley-Blackwell), pp. 5–20. Discusses the social and historical milieu of Socrates' trial and execution.

Plato. (2002) *Five Dialogues*, 2nd Edition, trans. G.M.A. Grube and J.M. Cooper (Indianapolis: Hackett). High-quality translation of *Euthypho, Apology, Meno, Crito*, and *Phaedo*.

Pritchard, D. (2014) 'What Is Knowledge? Do We Have Any?' in M. Chrisman and D. Pritchard (eds.) *Philosophy for Everyone* (New York: Routledge), pp. 21–36. A brief and highly accessible chapter on epistemology.

Spiller, H., J. Hale, and J. Z. de Boer. (2003) 'Questioning the Delphic Oracle,' *Scientific American*, vol. 289, pp. 67–73. Influential but controversial archeological study aiming to establish that the Pythian inhaled a noxious vapor emanating from underground in Delphi.

Taylor, C. (1998) *Socrates: A Very Short Introduction* (Oxford: Oxford University Press.) Brief introduction to the thought of Socrates; more focused on philosophical questions as compared with Johnson.

Advanced Further Reading

Bowden, H. (2005) *Classical Athens and the Delphic Oracle* (Cambridge: Cambridge University Press). Advanced scholarly text explaining relations between Athenian culture and politics and operations at Delphi.

Fontenrose, J. (1978) *The Delphic Oracle: Its Responses and Operations* (Berkeley: University of California Press). Detailed discussion of archeological evidence concerning Delphi.

Kraut, R. (1992) *The Cambridge Companion to Plato* (Cambridge: Cambridge University Press). Collection of articles on Plato by leading contemporary scholars.

Pritchard, D. (2009) *Knowledge* (London: Palgrave Macmillan). Accessible and self-contained introduction to epistemology.

Reeve, C. (1989) *Socrates in the Apology: An Essay on Plato's Apology of Socrates* (Indianapolis: Hackett). Influential study of many of the central philosophical ideas playing a role in the *Apology*.

Internet Resources

Green, 'The Examined Life,' in *Wi-Phi* (http://wi-phi.org). A brief animated video briefly setting forth the core ideas of this chapter.

Nails, D. 'Socrates,' in *The Stanford Encyclopedia of Philosophy* (http://plato.stanford.edu/entries/socrates/). Accessible and informative overview of Socrates' life and thought.

2　Descartes' Essence

Introduction

What is now termed the Modern era in the Western philosophical tradition has its inception with René Descartes (1596–1650) and his attempt to place science on a firmer foundation than it had rested on before. To dramatize the need to do so, he raises doubts about our ability to know even the most basic truths, and from there proceeds to respond to these doubts while developing a philosophical system that came to be one of the best-known versions of rationalism. In the course of this, Descartes articulates a striking view about the mind's relation to the body, as well as our knowledge of our own minds.

Some Radical Doubts

Have you ever woken up from a dream to be told by someone else that you had cried out in your sleep? If so, it would seem that at least during this dream you believed that something bad was either taking place or was about to do so. Maybe you dreamed that on your way home with your friends after seeing your favorite band, the Alpaca Lips, you were chased by hipsters threatening to drown you in a vat of kombucha; or in spite of your distaste for facial hair, you dreamed that you looked in the mirror and saw that you had grown an extravagant lumberjack beard. No wonder you cried out!

In some cases, we dream while remaining aware, on some level, that we are doing so. In others, such as the one I just imagined, we seem to believe that what is happening in the dream is real. That would help explain why you cried out. Philosophers have been interested in dreams for a long time, and for a number of reasons. One reason is that if it is possible to have a dream that you believe, while it is occurring, to be real, that possibility might make you reflect on what is happening to you *right now*: after all, you *could* be dreaming that you are reading a book called *Know Thyself: The Value and Limits of Self-Knowledge*. I would like to think that this would not be as scary a dream as the one in which you are being chased by hipsters on your way home from the Alpaca Lips concert, but perhaps that is not for me to say. Be that as it may, we are in a position to ask the following question: given that in the past you have had a dream in which you were sure, at the time it was occurring, that it was real; given that this has occurred in the past, what can you do to rule out that your *current* experience is not just another equally convincing dream?

This might seem like a silly question. After all, can't you pinch yourself to ensure that you're awake? Well, you might try that, but couldn't you just as easily have a dream in which you are pinching yourself to see if you're dreaming? There you are lying in bed, dreaming that you're pinching yourself to see if you're awake or dreaming, and your roommate hears you yell out, "Ouch!" Surely this could happen. But if that is so, then we may also conclude that while you may *feel* sure that you are not dreaming right now, it is not so clear that you can find a rational basis for that confidence. The problem I am raising is a form of what philosophers call *skepticism*. Skepticism in philosophy poses a challenge to our ability to know the things we take ourselves to know. As such, it is a topic within the broader area of epistemology, which is the study of the forms and bases of knowledge, wisdom, belief, conviction, understanding, and related notions. Since our concern in this book is with knowledge directed toward the self, it will be useful first to consider some general epistemological questions and the skeptical concerns they bring with them.

To prepare for that task, let us distinguish two ways of knowing about one's own mind, as well as three general sorts of things that minds contain. For the first of these, consider two ways in which I might come to realize that I am angry. One is the more common, where for instance something makes me angry, and my anger is obvious to me because I can "catch" myself feeling that emotion. We may call this the *first-personal*, or *introspective*, way of knowing about one's state of mind. But I might also find out that I am angry by means that others might use to find out that I am: I happen to see myself in the mirror, and notice—what I had not been aware of before—my clenching fists, bulging vein on my forehead, scowling expression, and the like. I might conclude from these indicators that I am angry, but if I do so, I am using the same evidence that others might use to learn about my emotional state. For this reason, we may describe this as a case of knowing about my state of mind in a *third-personal*, or *extrospective*, way. In Chapter 4 we will consider the question whether there could be states of one's mind that can only be known in a third-personal way.

These introspective and extrospective methods are two different ways of knowing about one's state of mind. It will also be useful at this point to think further about the kinds of thing a mind might contain. States of mind are a subset of the features that a self might have. One individual may be described by character traits such as being introverted, kind to animals, and short-tempered; another might be described as domineering toward some and sycophantic toward others. Such traits as these are aspects of a person, but are not normally thought of as states of one's mind. Instead, they are features that tend to produce such states of mind and the behaviors associated with them. For instance, an introvert might find, as he enters a room full of people talking animatedly, that he wants to move to a quiet corner and pay attention to the cat lounging there. So too, a short-tempered person might feel angry as he finds that he must wait in a long line to board a bus. Wanting to play with a cat and feeling angry about a long wait are both examples of mental states in the sense that we will focus on here. So is believing that something is so, and undergoing an experience such as feeling a pain or hearing the sound of thunder. To add some system to this variety of mental states, we will distinguish among cognitive, affective, and experiential states as follows:

Cognitive states: these are states of mind whose business is to process information, and that represent the world as being a certain way. Examples are beliefs (such as that grass is green, or that the capital of Mongolia is Ulaanbaatar), conjectures (such as that the puppy might have stolen your missing sock), or even guesses (such as that your poker opponent is bluffing). As a first approximation, memories and expectations are special cases of beliefs directed toward the past and future respectively.

Affective states: this category includes both emotions and moods. Examples of the latter are feelings of anxiety, exuberance, or gloom. While we can sometimes point to a cause of a mood, there is not always an answer to the question what one's mood is *about*. If I have consumed too much coffee, I may become anxious even though there need not be an answer to the question what I am anxious about. (A mood, as philosophers like to say, can have a *cause* without having an *object*.) Or hearing a lot of gloomy music might put you in a gloomy mood. You *might* be gloomy about something in particular, but your gloom need not have an object to be genuine, or even to produce a significant change in your behavior. By contrast, with an emotion, there is always an answer to the question what it is about, even if the person in whom that emotion is occurring has trouble articulating that answer. Imagine someone who says she is feeling hopeful. If we ask her what she is hopeful about, we would not expect her to reply, "Well, I'm just feeling hopeful, but not about anything in particular." That hardly makes sense, and if she sticks by that answer, it would seem more reasonable to describe her state of mind as one of general optimism or exuberance rather than hope. For hope, it seems, always requires that there be an answer to the question what one is hopeful about. So too for fear, anger, pride, resentment, and the other emotions.

Experiential states: these are states of mind that have a character associated with one or more of the senses. Imagine biting into a fresh slice of lemon. It is very sour, and might cause you to make a funny face. The juices in your mouth lead you to have a sensory experience exhibiting what is known as a *qualitative character*: there is a distinctive way that lemon tastes that is different from how orange, pineapple, or for that matter chocolate tastes. So too for the color you experience when you look at a red apple in good light, or the tactile experience you undergo when you pet a cat. Multiple sensory modalities might be activated at once: as you climb a flowering carob tree there will be tactile experience as your hands grasp a branch, olfactory experience as you smell the carob, as well as visual, auditory, and proprioceptive experiences.

All three types of psychological state—cognitive, affective, and experiential—share two further features. First of all, they are all types of state that can be known by introspection. While, as we will see in Chapter 4, some particular instances of, say, anger, might be closed to introspection due to being unconscious, at least in typical cases, I can also undergo anger in such a way as to know about it by introspecting. So too, I am usually cognizant of my own beliefs, expectations, and hypotheses, and am usually aware of whether I am smelling the aroma of oranges or hearing the sound of an airplane passing overhead.

Second, it would seem that psychological states always belong to the mind of some person or other. It does not seem possible, for instance, for a taste of lemon to simply float free of anyone's consciousness. Rather, a taste of lemon is always an experience that an individual, though not necessarily a human being, is undergoing. You can, I hope, see similar reasons for saying the same thing about affective and cognitive states: no happiness without its being the happiness of someone, and no beliefs that do not belong to a particular believer.[1]

Nothing guarantees that a mind will contain all three types of psychological state. If machines such as computers can have minds, perhaps they could possess cognitive, but neither affective nor experiential states. Likewise, some non-human animals might have experiential but neither cognitive nor affective states: perhaps a millipede has experiences afforded it by its sensory organs, but it seems doubtful that it has cognition or affect. So too, we can at least imagine a being with cognitive and experiential states, but no affective states: this is perhaps a part of what *Star Trek* asks us to imagine about Mr. Spock. Accordingly, in what follows we will think of human minds as normally containing cognitive, affective, and experiential states, but will not assume that all minds must contain all three, or even two out of these three.

René Descartes (1596–1650) was a mathematician, physicist, and philosopher who set out to establish a firm foundation for a new science that would be more rigorous than what had been dominant for centuries. To that end, he begins his book, *Meditations on First Philosophy*, with the question, what certain foundation can he find on which he can base all his beliefs? Is there anything of which he can be absolutely and justifiably sure? His initial answer to this question sounds pessimistic. For as we have just seen, I can even doubt, as I write these words, that I am sitting on a red couch even though my senses (visual, tactile, etc.) tell me that I am sitting on a couch and that it is a red one: I may after all just be having a vivid dream in which I am sitting on a red couch writing words on a laptop computer, with a large, brown dog snoozing at my feet, and so forth. Descartes dramatizes the point by remarking that for all he knows, there might be an Evil Genius of some kind who uses supernatural powers to produce illusions and hallucinations in him at every opportunity. We can make a similar point without any appeal to the supernatural by imagining the possibility that a neuroscientist has secretly anaesthetized you and hauled you into his laboratory. He has figured out a method to stimulate your central nervous system (CNS) in such a way as to bring about in you just the experiences you *would* have if you were experiencing the world normally. You have the *experience* of standing on a crowded subway platform waiting for your train to arrive as you head to work on a rainy Thursday morning, but perhaps that is just the result of the neuroscientist stimulating various parts of your CNS. You might have the experience of eating an egg salad sandwich, or taking a shower; but in principle these experiences too can be synthesized by a sufficiently clever and resourceful neuroscientist.

By this point the form of skepticism Descartes has raised has become quite radical. If we can't banish it, then it would seem to call into question pretty much everything we believe. However, Descartes also observes that even if he cannot be sure that he has hands, is awake, or is even a human being, it does seem that he can be sure that he is *having thoughts*. I am having the thoughts that I am sitting on a red couch, that it is sunny outside, and that my legs are crossed. Whether those thoughts accurately represent anything outside themselves, we have yet to be sure about. We can, however, be sure that we are having thoughts of some kind. But what follows from the fact that I am having a thought? We noticed above that there can be no "free floating" psychological states. A thought, mood, emotion, or experience must be a thought, mood, emotion, or experience had by some mind or other. But then it follows from the premise that I am having a thought, that there is an "I" who is having that thought. Descartes expresses this with the following line of reasoning:

1.   I am thinking (*cogito*).
     therefore (*ergo*)
2.   I exist (*sum*).

That is, from the premise that he is thinking, Descartes infers that he must also exist. This is known as the *Cogito argument*, which is among the more famous arguments in the Western philosophical tradition.

Notice that in using "I," in both the premise and conclusion of his argument, Descartes is not assuming that the word refers to a mind that possesses all three types of psychological properties (cognitive, affective, experiential), or any other types of property for that matter. All Descartes can know so far is that he has thoughts, and that he exists as a mind, in whatever manner is a bare minimum for the existence of minds.

God, Evil, and Clear and Distinct Perception

In the Second Meditation, then, Descartes gives a powerful argument for the conclusion that he exists. He next turns to trying to see what else he can establish about himself with certainty. He notices that he has such thoughts as, "I seem to be sitting in a chair." Now, he has yet to prove that there is no Evil Genius, and so cannot be sure that his experience of sitting in a chair is not illusory. However, it would appear that he can be sure that he *seems* to be sitting in a chair. So too, consider the following famous image, known as the Müller-Lyer Illusion:

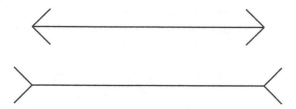

Diagram 2.1 The Müller-Lyer Illusion

Even if you know that the two lines are of the same length (and if you're in any doubt, just measure them), it will still most likely *seem* to you as if they are of different lengths. So too, Descartes will agree that it seems to him as if he is awake, sitting in a chair, or smoking a pipe, even if he is not in fact doing any of these things. What he concludes is that in addition to the fact that he exists (as established by the *Cogito argument*), he can also be sure how things seem to him. Further, these "seemings" often take the form of contemplating visual images, such as the image of a chair, the sensation of pipe smoke wafting through his nostrils, and the so forth. What is more, Descartes notices that he also sometimes forms intentions, makes judgments, and doubts things. He takes these all to be forms of thinking. He sums up what he has learned so far as follows:

> But what, then, am I? A thing that thinks. What is that? A thing that doubts, understands, affirms, denies, wills, refuses, and that also imagines and senses.
> (1993, p. 20)

It is easy enough to see how doubting, understanding, affirming, denying, willing, and refusing are forms of thinking. One might, for instance, engage in the mental action of affirming or denying by saying, in the privacy of one's thoughts, "I affirm (deny) that such and such proposition is true." So too one might say to oneself, "I will that I shall do so and so," or "I shall refuse to do so and so." But in what way are imagining and sensing forms of thinking? Part of Descartes' answer is that just as it is I who will, so too it is I who imagine, and likewise it is I who sense, even if I am still in the grip of the Evil Genius and so what I sense does not represent anything outside my own mind. Further, for Descartes, *seeming* to see, hear, taste, or smell something is what, properly speaking, sensing is. And he would seem to have a point if we think of sensing as a matter of undergoing sensations, which of course is something we may do even if we are being deceived about how things are outside our minds.

Descartes hopes to move beyond these insights about his own nature to further conclusions, including those that might help him gain knowledge of the world outside of his mind. As a starting point, Descartes observes that in general, ideas contain an inherent duality: when I have an idea, it occurs both as a mental phenomenon within me, and represents, or purports to represent, something outside me. My idea of the sun, for instance, is not massive, whereas the sun itself is. Further, my idea of God represents something external to me that is omniscient, omnipotent, and possesses any other perfections it is possible to possess. Something must have caused me to have that idea, Descartes will urge; and he makes the further, surprising suggestion that the only kind of entity that could have produced such an idea in me was something that itself had all possible perfections. Nothing else could have had enough of what Descartes terms "objective reality" to produce in me an idea of a being with all possible perfections. That is to say that the only thing that could have caused my idea of God, was God himself! (1993, p. 26).

Scholars and students have debated Descartes' line of reasoning here for centuries. I would guess that you can think of other possible sources of Descartes' idea of God that might challenge the conclusion he draws about its source. However we will not need to dwell on the cogency of Descartes' argument. Instead, what matters for our purposes is that Descartes believes that just by introspecting on his own idea of God, he can infer the existence of that being. In this respect, Descartes thinks he can derive a much more dramatic conclusion from his idea of God than he can from his ideas of, for instance, a tropical vacation, an incredibly high skyscraper, or a perpetual-motion machine. For by introspecting, and then considering and ruling out other possible explanations of the presence in his mind of what he treats as the idea of an "infinite substance," Descartes draws a *theistic* conclusion, that is, the conclusion that God exists.[2]

Descartes now moves from this theistic conclusion to what appears to be a novel way of acquiring new knowledge. To see how this works, consider the nature of evil. Some evils have primarily to do with suffering, such as when a tsunami drowns thousands of people. Others concern intentional wrongdoing, such as when one person deliberately belittles another about the way they look or their sexual orientation. Yet a third kind of evil flows from a person's failing to live up to a certain standard even when their failing to do so does not harm anyone else. A person blessed with musical talent might fail to cultivate that talent because she can't be bothered to put in the effort to do so. After all, long hours of practicing, ego-bruising lessons with a demanding teacher, and nerve-wracking public performances are all challenging, and many of us would prefer to avoid all the trouble and stress. On the other hand, a young musician might be assured by numerous experts that she does have a talent to cultivate. If she chooses not to do so, and instead takes a less demanding path in life rather than risk the possibility of failure, it is natural to feel that a considerable opportunity has been lost. What a tragedy to waste such talent, we may feel.

It seems an evil that this young musician's talent has gone to waste without her even making an effort to cultivate it. So too, it seems an evil for someone to commit an error in coming to a conclusion based on insufficient evidence. Such a faulty reasoner has failed to live up to her intellectual as opposed to artistic potential. Perhaps being in error is not as drastic an evil as murdering someone or willfully destroying property, but it is still something we would wish to avoid, whereas by contrast, gaining knowledge seems a good—an achievement to be valued.

Taking himself to have established that error is a kind of evil, Descartes next notices that since God has all perfections, he must be, among other things, maximally benevolent. This means that God will never willfully cause evil. Instead, if there is evil in the world, that evil would seem to have to be due to human choice rather than to the will of God. And while it may not be that when we make an error, we are deliberately doing so, it does seem that we often fall into error as a result of being less vigilant than we could have been in forming our opinions: we were rash in our calculations or in evaluation of the evidence, or used faulty instruments in gathering data; we engaged in some wishful thinking, or failed to consider possible challenges to the view that we were leaning toward, and so forth.

Error, Descartes infers, must be our own fault, never God's. But if that is right, then it would also seem that if we are doing our "epistemic best," that is, drawing conclusions only after the most painstaking and rigorous investigation of which we are capable, then those conclusions must be correct. For if they are incorrect, then they would constitute a case of error, and thus evil, that is not our fault. The only alternative is that they are God's fault. But that would be a case of an evil for which God is responsible, and this, Descartes feels sure, cannot happen. (Remember that God is benevolent to the highest degree possible.) As a result, any conclusions I reach in the course of doing my epistemic best, must be correct.

Descartes crystallizes this line of thought with what he calls *clear and distinct perception*, which is his label for a thought process in which one is being as vigilant as one can possibly be in drawing one's conclusions. He even goes so far as to formulate what we might think of as a rule of inference. In logic we often use rules of inference such as:

Either P is true or Q is true.
P is not true;
ergo,
Q is true.

Or

If P is true, then Q is true.
P is true;
ergo,
Q is true.

Similarly, Descartes proposes another rule of inference, namely:

> I clearly and distinctly perceive that P;
> *ergo*,
> P.

So, for instance, imagine you contemplate the possibility that two entities A and B could exist independently of one another. You think long and hard about that possibility, making sure that it contains no hidden contradictions. That done, you may conclude that you've clearly and distinctly perceived that it is possible for entities A and B to exist separately from one another. Then, on the strength of the third rule of inference displayed above, you may infer that it *is* possible for A and B to exist independently of one another. Likewise, if you clearly and distinctly perceive that it is not possible for A and B to exist separately, then A and B are necessarily identical. Let us call this type of inference the *Clear & Distinct Perception Rule*, or C&D Rule for short. It will be important in our discussion below of Descartes' view of the relation of the mind to the body.

Perception that is not clear and distinct Descartes calls obscure and confused. An important example that Descartes offers of obscure and confused perception is our naïve view about colors, smells, tastes, and other sensory properties of objects around us. According to Descartes, we naïvely think that what we normally refer to as a red apple has, as one of its features, the property of being red. Descartes, however, will urge that careful reflection on the matter reveals that colors are not characteristics of objects, but rather are only the results of those objects interacting with our sensory organs. So too for smell, textures, tastes, sounds, and other sensory characteristics. These are not "primary qualities" of objects (in the way that shape, location in space and time, extension, and direction of movement are) but rather are "secondary qualities"—which are in a sense within us rather than in the objects themselves.

Descartes rightly emphasizes that it may not be easy to eschew obscure and confused thinking and replace it with clear and distinct ideas only. After all, the idea that redness for instance is not in the apple, but rather in our minds, seems counter to everyday experience. It might take years of practice and exacting meditation on the proper attitude of the mind before our thinking becomes clear and distinct. So too, even if our initial impulse is to suppose that stars we see at night are small, familiarizing ourselves with modern astronomy requires setting aside that impulse and recognizing that each of these stars is enormous. In spite of the difficulty of the journey toward clear and distinct perception, Descartes holds that we must traverse this arduous path if we are to make serious progress in understanding ourselves and the world around us.

Two Kinds of Substance

Descartes puts his view about clear and distinct perception to good use in the Sixth (and final) Meditation. He here raises a question about how his mind relates to his body. Is he a partly or wholly material thing, or something of a different kind? To work toward an answer, Descartes points out that he can imagine existing disembodied. You probably can as well. After all, even if you are not a theist, you can still imagine being in, say, a horrific, fatal car accident, and then soon afterward find yourself departing from your mangled body. You may even contemplate the possibility of disembodied existence carefully, and, as Descartes would predict, not find any subtle contradiction hidden in such a hypothesis. But if this is right, that is, if you do your epistemic best and find no contradiction lurking in the idea that you *could* exist disembodied, then something rather surprising follows. For from the premise that

I clearly and distinctly perceive that I can exist disembodied,

we may infer, by the C&D Rule,

I can exist disembodied.

This might not seem like a very momentous conclusion. But note that if entities x and y are identical, then they have all the same properties. Thus if Mark Twain is identical with Samuel Clemens, then any property one has (such as the property of being the author of *The Adventures of Tom Sawyer*), the other has as well. So too, if the Morning Star is identical with the Evening Star, then they share all their properties. Conversely, if one has a property that the other lacks, then they are not identical. This idea, that if x and y are identical, then they have exactly the same properties, is known as the *Indiscernibility of Identicals*. (It is not to be confused with the more controversial doctrine of the Identity of Indiscernibles.)

Consider, accordingly, the relationship between your mind and your body. (By "body" here I mean to refer to your entire physical being, including your brain, the rest of your central nervous system, bones, skin, and so forth.) According to our thought experiment above about surviving the destruction of your body, your mind seems to have the following property, namely that of being *capable of existing without your body*. On the other hand, your body does not have that property: your body certainly is not capable of existing without itself! But now note what follows: your mind has a property that your body lacks, namely, the property of being capable of existing without your body. From the Indiscernibility of Identicals, we may infer that your mind and body are not identical.

This conclusion may seem unremarkable. However, the same reasoning can be used to deduce that your mind is not identical with any physical substance whatever—your brain, your frontal cortex, your pre-frontal cortex, your favorite computer, what have you. The result is an instance of the philosophical doctrine known as *dualism*. Dualism is an answer to the question, what kinds of things are there? One answer is *monist*, and holds that there is only one kind of thing. The best-known form of monism is materialistic monisn (usually just called materialism for brevity), according to which the only kind of things that exist are material objects—atoms, their components, and the forces governing them, such as electromagnetic forces. Dualism is opposed to materialistic monism by virtue of holding that even after accounting for all the physical things in the world, you still have not accounted for all the things that exist. The reason, the dualist will say, is that in addition to all the material things that exist, there are also non-material things, such as minds. This dualist position is precisely the one that Descartes aims to establish with his argument involving the possibility of disembodied existence, the Indiscernibility of Identicals, and the like.

We have had to work hard to develop the dualist position at which Descartes finally arrives, but I hope you agree that it was worth the effort. For if Descartes is right, then physics, chemistry, neuroscience, and other sciences will never give a complete description of the world. These sciences will always leave out information about minds which, if Descartes is correct, are non-physical and thus beyond the reach of the physical, chemical, or biological sciences. What is more, each person knows her or his own mind with unshakeable certainty. Descartes puts the point as follows:

> Since I now know that even bodies are not, properly speaking, perceived by the senses or by the faculty of imagination, but by the intellect alone . . . I manifestly know that nothing can be perceived more easily and more evidently than my own mind.
>
> (1993, p. 23)

Ever since our brush with the Delphic oracle, we have learned to be on the lookout for the precise meaning of words. Accordingly, strictly speaking the claim that nothing can be perceived more easily and more evidently than my own mind does not itself entail that I can perceive my own mind with any success whatsoever. After all, perhaps nothing at all can be perceived easily and evidently! (Remember, the claim that no one is wiser than Socrates does not imply that Socrates is wise.) However, it does appear that Descartes intends the statement just quoted to imply that he can perceive his own mind with great accuracy. For, you will recall, he has set out to place the new science he envisions on a firm foundation that is not subject to skeptical challenges. He starts with knowledge of his own mind, and proposes to build out from there. This project would have no hope of success if he were not able to know his own mind with certainty.

Bitters and Sweets of Dualism

Descartes' brand of dualism is a powerful view, and it has had countless defenders and detractors in the centuries since he first formulated it. All too often, however, those criticizing the view are content to use "Cartesian dualism" as a term of abuse rather than explaining how and why Descartes' argument for it goes wrong, if in fact it does. In other cases, philosophers have simply asserted a materialist position without taking the measure of Descartes' arguments for a contrary view.

For instance, the French physician, philosopher, and libertine Julian Offray de La Mettrie (1709–1751) wrote *Man a Machine*, in which he argues that human beings differ only in degree of complexity from non-human animals as well as complex machines. In a characteristic passage, La Mettrie writes,

> The human body is a clock, a huge and complex and finely designed clock. How well designed? Well, if the cog-wheel that marks the seconds happens to stop, the one that marks the minutes goes on turning, as does the wheel marking the quarter-hours; and similarly with the others, when the first ones are halted by rust or some other cause. For we know—don't we?—that when several blood-vessels are blocked, that doesn't stop or suspend the main movement in the heart, which is like the mainspring of the machine.
>
> (La Mettrie, 1994, p. 46)

To his credit, elsewhere in his essay La Mettrie attempts to give materialist explanations of imagination, emotion, attention, and language. However, he nowhere explains where Descartes' argument for dualism goes wrong. To do so, La Mettrie would have to explain either how one of the premises of Descartes' argument is dubious, or how the inference from those premises to the dualistic conclusion is fallacious. La Mettrie does neither of these things, and for this reason does not offer a fully satisfactory alternative to the dualist position.

To clarify the challenge that we face, let us observe that Descartes' argument depends on a small number of premises, each of which is hard to gainsay. As a result, if you are going to reject his dualistic conclusion, you need to explain where that argument errs: do you deny the Indiscernibility of Identicals (good luck!), or that your mind is capable in principle of existing disembodied (really?!), or that the argument from these premises does not in fact validly entail its conclusion (show why!). Each of these options is daunting, but to make some headway, let us first consider some puzzling consequences of the dualistic position. Doing so will help us get our bearings as we try to figure out an intellectually satisfying response to Descartes' dualistic argument. So here are two objections to this position, which concern the interaction of mind and body, and our ability to know minds other than our own. I shall discuss each of these problems in turn.

Mind-Body Interaction

If a mind is not identical with anything physical, it would have to be a non-physical substance. But that raises the question, how could a non-physical substance interact with anything physical? On the one hand, it seems like mental events cause physical changes all the time. I decide I am thirsty, and so form an intention to pick up the glass of water on the table before me and take a sip; then, sure enough, up goes the glass to my lips. That would appear to be an example of a mental event (deciding to take a drink) bringing about a physical change (moving the glass to my lips). So too, a physical event can bring about a mental change: the drinking of that water can, it seems, bring about a mental change in me, such as a feeling of comfort resulting in the quenching of my thirst.

This all seems almost too obvious to be worth mentioning. However, it is not at all clear how something non-physical can effect a physical change, or vice versa. We tend to think that when a physical change occurs, it is because something else physical has brought it about: the water boils because it was heated, the glass breaks because it was hit very hard against the wall, the volcano erupted because the lava inside became too pressurized. However, if Descartes is correct in his view about the difference between mind and body, this is not entirely true: some physical changes have non-physical causes. The reason is that according to dualism, mental events are non-physical. As such, Cartesian dualism seems to have to deny a principle that you might, independently, have found attractive, namely that the physical world is "causally closed."

The Causal Closure of the Physical

Every physical event that has a cause, has a cause that is itself physical.

The Causal Closure of the Physical would seem to be among the background presuppositions of any serious physics textbook, for instance. However, if Descartes' is correct in his dualistic position, then he will, it seems, have to deny the Causal Closure of the Physical. That seems quite a cost to pay in order to adhere to dualism.

Does Descartes' dualism strictly contradict the Causal Closure of the Physical? One might try to answer this question by asking the further question whether mental and physical phenomena can run parallel to each other without ever interacting causally. Scientists often warn us that correlation does not imply causation. (An example makes the point clear: falling asleep with one's shoes on is correlated with waking up with a headache. But it would be a mistake to infer that sleeping with one's shoes on is what caused the headache; instead, the state you were in when you went to bed is probably what caused both your headache and your forgetting to take off your shoes!)

So perhaps my desire for a sip of water only *seems* to bring about the physical change of water being brought to my lips; but in fact for some reason, be it good luck or some other cause, the one event only happened to be followed by the latter without being caused by it. Such a hypothesis would allow Descartes' dualism to remain consistent with Causal Closure. It would, however, raise a further question: what accounts for the fact that on countless occasions, both in my own life and in that of others (both human and non-human animals), mental events tend to be followed by physical changes that are either beneficial to our bodies (slaking of thirst, ingestion of food), or precede further mental events that conform with what we are aiming to achieve (cessation of thirst or hunger)? In resolving one mystery, perhaps the defender of Descartes has created another one no less severe.

Knowledge of Other Minds

Here is a different challenge for the dualist. Common sense has it that we regularly know a good deal about what is going on in the minds of others. Particularly for those whom you know well, such as close friends and family members, you probably make frequent attributions of thoughts, emotions, and other mental contents. You effortlessly recognize that, say, your mother is irritated with you for not dropping her off at her Taekwondo class on time, and you instantly see that your niece is thrilled with the toy that you gave her in celebration of Arbor Day. Attributions of mental states to others would seem to be part of our everyday social competence, and those unable to make such attributions reliably may be severely handicapped as social beings.

Common sense, then, tells us that we often, and reliably, attribute mental states to others. But if Descartes' dualism is correct, this fact would seem mysterious indeed. After all, when a computer performs a process such as analyzing data, we feel sure that if we wanted to and had the expertise, we could open up the machine and see the physical basis for that process. So too, we know that if a tree is looking unhealthy, an arborist could examine it more carefully and probably find the cause: a fungus is eating away at the bark, or gypsy moths are devouring all its leaves. We expect to verify or refute our hypotheses about the causes of changes in things around us by looking inside of them and seeing what is going on at the physical level. But if Descartes' dualism is correct, nothing of the sort is possible when we make attributions of mental states to others. After all, if dualism is correct, then even if we use our most sophisticated fMRI techniques to examine what is going on in a person's brain, doing so will not settle what is going on in her mind.

The problem, then, is that while we believe ourselves to regularly and reliably make attributions of mental states to others, dualism seems to imply that such a thing should not be possible. Now, as was the case with the problem of mind-body interaction, not everyone will take the problem of other minds to be a decisive refutation of Descartes' position. Someone defending him might instead clench her teeth and reply as follows:

> Well, as a matter of fact, while I can know the contents of my own mind by means of introspection, and with certainty, things really are much more speculative when it comes to other minds. We are after all sometimes wrong about what others are thinking or feeling. So perhaps all we can ever hope for is to form *hypotheses* about the contents of other minds, but never achieve knowledge about them.

If this response is correct, other minds really aren't knowable—all we can do is speculate about them—whereas each of us can be certain about the contents of her own mind. Further, if this means that common sense, according to which we do know a great deal about other people's minds, is mistaken, then it would not be the first time common sense has gone wrong. After all, many thousands of years ago, before any sophisticated navigation or astronomy, common sense would not have taken the Earth to be spherical. So too, in the Middle Ages, before the birth of modern medicine and psychology, common sense would have taught us that people's moods are largely caused by the kinds of vapors that are flowing through their veins. (It had yet to be discovered by William Harvey in the seventeenth century that the veins are full of blood and thus have no room for vapor.) Perhaps, the defender of Descartes will now say, common sense may well also wrong about our knowledge of other minds.

We have considered two objections to Descartes' dualist position, and have contemplated in response to each such objection a reply that someone might make on Descartes' behalf. At this point, however, if you have spent any time learning about modern neuroscience, you may be feeling a bit frustrated and eager to offer a third objection. For modern neuroscience seems to show that thinking, emoting, and experiencing are all processes occurring in the central nervous system. Every week, it seems, a careful reader of the news will encounter yet another article reporting a discovery from a laboratory somewhere in the world showing the location within the brain of, say, musical cognition, or anger and fear, or memory. How, one might ask, could thinking, emoting, and experiencing possibly *not* be physical processes occurring in our CNS?

If the above line of (exasperated) reasoning at all captures your thoughts at this point, you are not alone. And you may indeed be right. Perhaps, instead of dualism, materialist monism is the more reasonable view of the relation of mind to body. However, it is one thing to *assert* materialist monism, as did critics of Descartes such as the English philosopher Thomas Hobbes (1588–1679) and, as we have seen, La Mettrie, and quite another to show exactly how Descartes' arguments for his dualistic position go wrong. As we have seen, in the Sixth Meditation, Descartes gives a powerful, surprisingly simple argument for his dualist position. Someone wishing to establish materialistic monism will only succeed in this task if she can explain where Descartes' reasoning erred. That is no small task, but it is one will we attempt in the next chapter.

Descartes' views about our knowledge of our own states of mind are allied with a larger project he was engaged in to place science on a firmer foundation than it had rested on before. His approach to self-knowledge is intriguing and tempting in its own right, however. For it does seem that if we are intimately in touch with anything, it is with our own psychological states. Yet the dualistic position with which this view of self-knowledge is allied seems controversial at best. Accordingly, in the next chapter we will turn to the question whether Descartes' powerful arguments for his dualistic position can legitimately be resisted. Along the way, we will begin to appreciate numerous respects in which the confidence we feel about our knowledge of our own minds merits some qualification. Challenges to our confidence about our knowledge of our own minds may come either from the existence of aspects of our minds of which we are not aware; or they might come from our desire to believe something about ourselves that may not be quite true. The former set of challenges brings up the topic of the unconscious, while the latter brings up the topic of self-deception.

First, however, we turn in the next chapter to a philosopher who tried to put his finger on where precisely Descartes' argument for dualism went wrong.

Chapter Summary

- René Descartes' writings were a major turning point in Western philosophy. He advocated a new method to make progress in the sciences, and employed his famous skepticism to dramatize the need for such a new approach.
- To understand Descartes' new methodology, we must also make sense of his theological commitments, including his views on God and evil, particularly as they pertain to Descartes' conception of error as a kind of evil. This in turn enables us to understand the doctrine of "clear and distinct perception."
- Descartes' reasoning raises skeptical questions, which call into doubt our claims to know the things we do. Some of these questions are radical, and might get us to doubt things that we take to be patently obvious.
- Descartes pays special attention to his ability to know his own mind. This in turn leads to what he takes to be a proof of his own existence, and to an argument for the distinctness of the mind and body.
- This dualistic conclusion is open to two famous objections, one pertaining to the causal interaction of mind and body, and the other concerning our ability to know the minds of others.
- There are two ways of knowing one's mind: introspective (also known as first-personal) and extrospective (also known as third-personal).
- The human mind is generally held to contain three kinds of states: cognitive, affective, and experiential. It is an open question whether all minds (including those of other species, those that have been created artificially, and those that might inhabit other regions of the universe) must contain all three kinds of mental states, and whether cognitive, affective, and experiential states exhaust the kind of state that any mind can possibly contain.
- Descartes set out to develop a new foundation for the sciences that would consist of principles of which we may be certain. Doing so required reassessing the merits of as many of his beliefs as possible.
- In the course of this reassessment, Descartes argues that he can be certain of his existence, as well as of the contents of his own mind. He proceeds from there to argue for the existence of God, and on that basis, to argue that everything that he clearly and distinctly perceives is true.
- Descartes provides a subtle and powerful argument in the Sixth Meditation that the mind and body are not just capable of existing separately, but that they are in fact distinct. This dualist position holds that the mind is not identical to any substance whatsoever.
- Dualism suggests unintuitive consequences, such as the conclusion that mind and body only *seem* to interact but do not in fact do so; and that it is not possible ever truly to know what is going on in any mind other than one's own.

Study Questions

1. Do you have any way of determining with certainty that you are not dreaming right now? Please explain your answer.
2. Could Descartes' *cogito* argument be used to prove the existence of fictional objects? (After all, you could write a story in which, say, Bugs Bunny notices that he is thinking, and infers that he exists!)
3. Could one adhere to Descartes' dualism but deny that minds and bodies ever truly interact? (It would be valuable if we could make such a view plausible, since that would prevent us from having to give up the Causal Closure of the Physical.)
4. Please explain Descartes' reasons for holding that a piece of wax has few of the properties that our common-sense ways of thinking ascribe to it.
5. Descartes appears to have a different conception of what is involved in knowing oneself, and, correspondingly, from living an examined life, from that of Socrates. How would you characterize the main differences between these two philosophers on these issues?

Notes

1. Philosophers concerned with art have noted that some human creations come close to offering cases of affective states that are not the property of any mind. Some pieces of music, for instance, even if purely instrumental and lacking in words, can be sad or exuberant. Also, later in this book we will consider a Buddhist approach that will challenge the idea that all psychological phenomena must occur in the mind of someone or other.
2. In this book we will define *theism* as the view that there exists a being with all possible perfections, where the perfections in question are usually thought to include such attributes as omniscience (knowing all that there is to know), omnipotence (being able to do everything that it is possible to do), omnibenevolence (being as good as it is possible to be), and omnipresence (being located in every place). Theism is neutral among different religious creeds, such as Islam, Judaism, and Christianity, all of which offer their followers particular ways of being theistic. One who believes that there does not exist an infinitely perfect being is known as an *atheist*. One who remains neutral on the question whether theism is correct is an *agnostic*.

Introductory Further Reading

Cottingham, J. (1992) *The Cambridge Companion to Descartes* (Cambridge: Cambridge University Press). A collection of high-quality scholarly essays examining Descartes' philosophy.

Descartes, R. (1993) *Meditations on First Philosophy*, 3rd Edition, ed. D.A. Cress (Indianapolis: Hackett). A compact and highly readable translation of the central text.

La Mettrie, J. (1994) *Man a Machine, and Man a Plant*, trans. R. Watson and M. Rybalka (Indianapolis: Hackett). Amusing and somewhat dogmatic defense of materialistic monism.

Sorell, T. (2000) *Descartes: A Very Short Introduction* (Oxford: Oxford University Press). Accessible and brief overview of the central tenets of Descartes' philosophical views.

Advanced Further Reading

Hobbes, T. (1651/1994) *Leviathan, With Selected Variants from the Latin Edition of 1668*, ed. E. Curley (Indianapolis: Hackett).

———. (1655/1981) *Part I of De Corpore*, trans. A. P. Martinich (New York: Abaris Books). These two works of Hobbes together formulate his materialist monist response to Cartesian dualism.

Secada, J. (2013) 'God and Meditation in Descartes' *Meditations on First Philosophy*,' in K. Detlefsen (ed.) *Descartes' Meditations: A Critical Guide* (Cambridge: Cambridge University Press), pp. 200–25. Defends the importance of both theism and meditative practice for understanding Descartes.

Stroud, B. (2008) 'Our Debt to Descartes,' in J. Broughton and J. Carriero (eds.) *A Companion to Descartes* (Hoboken, NJ: Wiley-Blackwell). Argues for the enduring importance of the skeptical challenges that Descartes raises in the early parts of the *Meditations*.

Williams, B. (1978) *Descartes: The Project of Pure Inquiry* (New York: Penguin). Classic critical exposition of some main features of Descartes' philosophy.

Wilson, M. (1978) *Descartes* (London: Routledge and Kegan Paul). Another classic discussion of Descartes; essential reading for anyone pursuing further study of the topic.

Internet Resources

Descartes' Major Works online, at *Early Modern Texts*. (www.earlymoderntexts.com/authors/descartes). Translation of Descartes that make a special effort to put his thoughts into contemporary, idiomatic prose.

The Descartes Web Project, directed by Patricia Easton (Claremont Graduate University). Containing an online copy of *The Passions of the Soul* in parallel texts of French and English. (http://net.cgu.edu/philosophy/descartes/index.html).

Newman, L. (2014) 'Descartes' Epistemology,' in E. N. Zalta (ed.) *The Stanford Encyclopedia of Philosophy* (https://plato.stanford.edu/entries/descartes-epistemology/). Rigorous but informative discussion of core aspects of Descartes' approach to knowledge.

Smith, K. (2014) 'Descartes' Life and Works,' in *Stanford Encyclopedia of Philosophy* (https://plato.stanford.edu/entries/descartes-works/). Excellent biographical and thematic overview.

3 Ryle's Re-casting of the "Mind/Body Problem"

Introduction

The current chapter focuses on a trenchant criticism that applies not only to Descartes but to the legacy that he bequeathed concerning how we ask questions about the relation of mind to body. This legacy has it that minds and bodies are both substances, and then asks whether these two kinds of substance are identical, distinct, or stand in some other relation to one another such as "emergence" or "supervenience" (both technical terms that we will not need to define here). We begin with an overview of some well-known forms of the movement known as behaviorism, and show that Gilbert Ryle's version of this project is more resilient and interesting for our current purposes than are those associated with, say, John Watson and B. F. Skinner. We then consider Ryle's charge that Descartes is not so much *mistaken* about the nature of the mind as he is *confused* about notions pertaining to mentality and intelligence. This is typified by Ryle's claim that Descartes' way of thinking about mentality commits him to a category mistake, and that the charge applies to other theories of mentality as well. We also consider ways in which Ryle advocates an early form of what is now called embodied cognition, as well as his surprising view that so-called privileged access is a matter of degree rather than of kind. In addition, Ryle was curiously dismissive of empirical investigations of mentality and intelligence, and we will prepare for discussion in later chapters of how experimental psychology might, contrary to Ryle's dismissal, deepen our insight into both mentality and our attempts to know our own minds.

Styles of Behaviorism

We saw in the last chapter that it is easy enough to assert materialistic monism in reply to dualism. However, when such responses were made in the seventeenth (Hobbes) and eighteenth (La Mettrie) centuries, they were made with little attempt to explain where Descartes' argument for his position goes wrong. Materialists such as Hobbes and La Mettrie might be correct in their rejection of the dualist framework, but we need to understand why they are correct if they are, and how a thinker as great as Descartes could have erred in reaching the conclusions that he did. The twentieth-century movement known as behaviorism offers a clue that will help us answer these questions.

If you have taken a course in psychology or the philosophy of mind, the idea that behaviorism might help us with a current problem may come as a surprise. In such courses, behaviorism is typically presented as an unfortunate episode in the history of the study of mind. Behaviorism was indeed beset by severe limitations, such as its inability to account for sophisticated forms of intelligence including that found in the realm of human language use. Yet we also need to distinguish among different varieties of behaviorism. For instance, some behaviorists were concerned to establish the fledgling field of psychology on a scientific foundation in order to give it credibility within European and American universities. For this purpose, the field's leaders famously insisted that because mental phenomena such as beliefs, desires, emotions, and experiences are not observable, reference to such phenomena should also be eschewed in psychological research. Instead, it was held, we should seek, test, and establish laws connecting stimuli of various kinds and the behavioral response they can elicit: under what conditions will a sound of one type, when paired with a reward such as food, produce a behavioral or physiological response in an organism even when the reward is no longer presented? Under what conditions will a reward elicit an organism's ability to negotiate its way through a maze? And so on. Let us call this *psychological behaviorism*, which itself has many sub-varieties.

By contrast with psychological behaviorism, *philosophical behaviorism* takes two forms, each quite different from the other. One form proposes to reduce mental phenomena to patterns of behavior. On such a view, we might take a sentence ascribing a mental state to an organism and translate it into a set of sentences that make reference only to behavior understood in the sense of publicly observable bodily movements. We may contrast this with philosophical behaviorism of a non-reductive kind, associated primarily with the work of the English philosopher Gilbert Ryle (1900–1976). Ryle is not concerned to place psychology on a scientific footing. Rather, his aim is to show that once we reflect carefully on our common-sense notions of mind, intelligence, and related notions, we will see that the dualistic picture inherited from Descartes is not so much incorrect as confused. We shall accordingly see that Ryle—unlike Hobbes and La Mettrie—has the means to show where Descartes' argument for his dualistic position goes awry.

Ryle, then, is not concerned to show that psychology can be made scientific. Rather, his concern is to answer the question, what is it to have mind, and his answer starts with the observation that mentality and intelligence are intimately bound up with one another. That is, it is difficult to see how a creature—human or otherwise—could be *completely* lacking in intelligence, and yet still have a mind. Instead, intelligence is at least a necessary condition of mentality. What is more, intelligence is a matter of acting, or being disposed to act in goal-achieving ways that are at least moderately successful. Doing so will generally require a responsiveness to one's environment, the ability to adapt to novel situations, and a tendency to choose methods that are, on average, efficient ways of reaching one's goals.

To see what Ryle is getting at here, consider the 1994 movie, *Forrest Gump*, directed by Robert Zemeckis. The protagonist, Forrest, seems superficially to have a mental disability, but in spite of this apparent disability manages to live an extraordinary life. For instance, he finds himself participating in, and sometimes even inspiring, significant historical events and movements of the 1960s and 1970s. Forrest is also the movie's narrator, and at a number of points in the story remarks that his mother always told him, "Stupid is as stupid does!" The thought here is that even if a person *seems* to be unintelligent, perhaps due to their slow speech or odd mannerisms, the quality of their mind should instead be assessed in terms of their ability to get along in life successfully. Forrest's challenge to us is that if you want to call him stupid, perhaps because of his unconventional behavior, you may reconsider that attitude once you take into account his many extraordinary achievements.

I suspect that if he had lived long enough to see the movie, Ryle would approve of Mr. Gump's point. He might even have gone on to expand upon it. First, Ryle might qualify Gump's point by saying, "Stupid is as stupid does, or tends to do." The reason for this qualification is that one can be stupid while doing nothing at all: just imagine a person who is fast asleep. It may still be true that *if* that person were to wake up, he would perform poorly on a wide variety of intelligence-demanding tasks. If so, then that is a very good reason for denying that he is intelligent. Further, Ryle would suggest an analogous remark we might make about possessing intelligence. He might for instance say,

Intelligent is as intelligent does, or tends to do.

Of course, one can also be intelligent while sleeping soundly. The fact that you are lying in bed, snoring away, does not show that you are not intelligent. What matters is that you are disposed to behave intelligently under the right conditions. To see a bit more clearly what this notion of being disposed to behave intelligently comes to, consider the humble salt shaker sitting unused in a cabinet. This item is full of salt, and it is clear that this salt is *soluble*. What this means, at least in part, is that if it *were* put in an unsaturated liquid, it *would* dissolve. This statement can be true even of a sample of salt that is perfectly dry and undissolved. So too, when we say that a liquid such as gasoline is flammable, we mean not that it is burning at this particular time. Instead, what we mean is that this sample of liquid is disposed to ignite: expose it to a match or spark, and a terrible conflagration will likely ensue.

Similarly, consider a good chess player. She is disposed to do the following sorts of things when playing chess: dominate the center of the board, make exchanges of pieces that favor her own, pursue strategies that are unexpected, "see" multiple moves ahead, and so on. She can be a good chess player—in the sense that she is disposed to do these kinds of things—even if right now she is washing dishes or horseback riding. We may go a step further as we consider how we might give a dispositional account of other qualities of mind:

Being a good bird spotter
Having a refined fashion sense
Being a whiz at quadratic equations
Being an excellent judge of horses
Having perfect pitch

Each of these descriptions refers to what Ryle would think of as qualities of mind, but they are also best understood in dispositional terms. Can you explain what kinds of disposition each characteristic implicitly refers to?

At this point we may glimpse Ryle's account of what it is to have a mind: it is a matter of being intelligent, and *that* means acting, or being disposed to act, in intelligent ways. Moreover, from this perspective, what counts as intelligent, and thus as having a mind, will depend a great deal on what kind of creature you are. Because of the different ecological niches in which these species live, bottlenose dolphin intelligence will be very different from the intelligence of a red-tailed hawk, which will in turn be different from the intelligence of a member of our own species in modern, post-industrial society. A red-tailed hawk moved out of its normal environment in such a way as to be unable to act intelligently (perhaps by being put in a small cage where it is unable to fly or hunt) will still *be* intelligent (at least for a period of time), but only in the dispositional manner that a sleeping chess master is intelligent. Likewise, a person can be adept at negotiating the complexities of a large corporation in a modern city while not having a clue as to how to start a fire or locate food in a trackless wilderness.

Ryle underlines the importance of skills in manifesting mentality with his famous distinction between *knowing how* and *knowing that*. The latter is the familiar state of mind, as discussed in the last chapter, consisting (at least) in having a justified, true belief in a proposition. Ryle reminds us that while the Western philosophical position has championed knowledge-that (what we have called *propositional knowledge*), it has largely ignored knowledge-how, which we in effect have already introduced with our examples of skills. Being a skilled bird spotter, for instance, may equally well be described as *knowing how* to identify a wide range of birds in different weather conditions and from various distances and vantage points. (Such know-how we will also call *ability knowledge*.) Ryle denies that philosophers have any reason for placing propositional knowledge on a higher level than ability knowledge. Indeed he contends that all propositional knowledge presupposes a level of ability knowledge. We will not assess that argument here. Instead, what is crucial for our purposes is that ability knowledge as manifested in skills is a form of intelligence, and thus a manifestation of mentality.

The Ghost in the Machine

One of Ryle's goals in *The Concept of Mind* is to show that a prevalent understanding of the mind and its relation to the body is confused in principle, rather than mistaken on one or more details. To prepare the ground for doing so, Ryle describes this prevalent understanding as consisting in a number of features. The overall position he calls the *Myth of the Ghost in the Machine*, which he describes as follows:

1.   Each normal person has both a body and a mind.
2.   A person's body can be destroyed while their mind, being non-physical, can continue to exist after his body's destruction.
3.   Bodies are located in space and time, and are subject to the same mechanical laws as are any other physical objects.
4.   Minds are located in time but not in space, and are not subject to those laws that govern physical objects. (Minds may instead be subject to a distinctive set of "psychological laws.")
5.   Each of us is intimately aware of the workings of her own mind. By contrast, we may at best form conjectures about the minds of others, and we have no definitive way of settling whether those conjectures are correct or not.
6.   Minds and bodies seem to interact, but the locus of that interaction can itself be neither mental nor physical.

(Ryle, 1949, pp. 11–12)

These six characteristics are natural developments of the dualistic picture that comes down to us from Descartes. Point 5, as you may recall from Chapter 2, seems to be mandated by the project that Descartes has of placing a new science on a firm footing: in order to have genuine scientific knowledge, we need to build out from an indubitable basis, and that basis will be one's knowledge of one's own mental states. It is only then, by reflecting on our idea of God, and application of the method of clear and distinct perception, that we can hope to move from introspective awareness to awareness of things in the world external to our minds.

Ryle points out that the proponent of this Ghost in the Machine doctrine might acknowledge that a person may undergo mental phenomena of which she is unaware; likewise, the proponent of this view may accept that a person might in some cases believe things about her state of mind that are incorrect. That is, the proponent of the Ghost story might acknowledge the existence of both unconscious mental phenomena and some form of self-deception. (We will return to explain these concepts shortly, but for now, let us construe an unconscious mental state as a mental state (and thus either a cognitive, affective, or experiential state) of which its owner is unaware; let us also construe self-deception as a case in which a person believes she is in a certain mental state that she is not in fact in.) However, such a proponent will insist that these are aberrant cases, whereas in paradigmatic cases a person can know with certainty what is occurring in her mind, and when she ascribes something to her own mind, she cannot fail to be correct.

Ryle acknowledges that the above six points together make a superficially attractive picture of the relation of mind-body; he even admits that at one time he accepted that picture! However, although this Ghost story possesses intuitive appeal, Ryle contends that it is also confused, and confused in a way that we can appreciate once we reflect on what common sense tells us about minds and those who possess them. Yet this way of arguing against the Ghost in the Machine Myth might seem peculiar. After all, in many respects points 1–6 seem to be part of common sense: one finds them supported in one way or another in much of the Judeo-Christian tradition, and one can even discern in the lyrics of much popular music sentiments that correspond to one or more of points 1–6.[1] Does this mean that Ryle will have to use one part of common sense to undermine another? If so, why could not the undermining just as easily go the other way?

I suspect that Ryle would answer this question by observing that while it is true that common sense has incorporated some or all of points 1–6 above, to the extent that it has, it has also been corrupted. Just as, in Medieval times, common sense might have been corrupted by a mistaken theory of the source of people's moods, to the extent that it would have been second-nature to describe a person's melancholic mood as being due to an excess of bile wafting through their veins; so too, Ryle might suggest, in present-day thought it is second nature to think of a person's mind as in principle independent of their entire physical being. It will, of course, be incumbent on Ryle to explain why this view of the mind is confused, and that is the task to which we now turn.

What Is a Category Mistake?

A person who commits a category mistake attempts to apply a concept to a thing of a logical type that it cannot coherently apply to. An example is as follows: suppose that you are a student at a university, and some relatives come to pay you a visit. After a day of touring around, your uncle proclaims,

> I've had a lovely time seeing the buildings, the quad, the students, the staff, and faculty. It was also great to see the Marching Band practicing, and I loved meeting your school mascot, the Fighting Sea Anemone. What fun! However, I never got a chance to see the University that I've heard so much about. Where might that be?

It would be natural to feel that your uncle is confused here. You would probably want to explain to him that the university is not another thing alongside all the buildings, faculty, students, and the like. Rather, it is nothing more than all those things working together with a reasonable degree of organization. Thinking that the university is a thing that one could touch or shake hands with is a confusion of levels—what Ryle calls a category mistake.

Another example: suppose your friends are preparing for a long bike journey. They tell you that they are going to ride across Romania in search of the Average Romanian Taxpayer. They suspect that this person lives somewhere northwest of Bucharest, but no matter what, they'll do their best to find her or him. You might reply by telling your friends that they are bound to fail in their task, even if the riding will be fun. For the Average Romanian Taxpayer is not an individual person of flesh and blood. Rather, the Average Romanian Taxpayer is an abstraction from all the flesh-and-blood, taxpaying Romanians that currently exist. What is more, even if the average taxpaying Romanian earns, say, the equivalent of €20,000, there need be no individual who earns exactly that amount. Thinking otherwise is to commit a category mistake.

Recall now that a premise of Descartes' argument for his dualistic conclusion is that one's mind is capable, at least in principle, of existing disembodied. (Remember too that this premise does not ask you to believe that you *will* survive the destruction of your body; only that it is a possibility.) Ryle would deny even this claim of possibility, pointing out that anything that did survive the complete destruction of its body would no longer have the ability to *behave*: no chess, no bird-spotting, no solving quadratic equations, no watercolor paintings of landscapes. But then there would be no basis for ascribing intelligence to this allegedly disembodied mind either. We have no idea what it would be for a disembodied mind to be a crafty chess player or an excellent judge of horses, simply because our notion of behavior is so tightly bound to what agents do with their bodies, including their eyes, hands, tongues, lips, and even brains. Accordingly, Ryle is in a position to reply to Descartes that while there are many things that we can imagine by virtue of forming a mental image or watching a cartoon, there is little reason to think all such events are genuinely possible. You might watch a movie that invites you to vividly imagine traveling into and modifying the past; or you might read a story about waking up to find that you've been turned into a large insect. In spite of the entertainment or artistic value of such stories, it does not follow that the things such stories ask us to imagine are genuinely possible—that they really could happen. What is more, when a fictional story does ask us to imagine a non-physical agent doing something, it always seems to do so by imagining that agent taking physical form: the Grim Reaper in Ingmar Bergman's *The Seventh Seal*, Satan in William Friedkin's *The Exorcist*, and the angels Damiel and Cassiel in Wim Wenders' *Wings of Desire*, all take physical form in the narrative in which they occur. Ryle might add that even if something were an immaterial substance, that would not be enough for it to have a mind, since there would be no way for this substance to act intelligently. As a student of mine once pointed out, one could be a Cartesian immaterial "mind" and still be dumb as a bag of hammers!

Ryle, then, will deny that one can clearly and distinctly perceive the possibility of a mind existing entirely disembodied, and his reason for this denial depends on a view of minds as being disposed to intelligent behavior, that is as loci of know-how. Here you might object: aren't there people who are quite unintelligent, and yet still have minds even if those minds are less impressive than those of Nobel Prize winners, poets, and astute judges of horses? If, you might continue, Ryle is implying that such obtuse people lack minds entirely, is he not going overboard and overstating his case in the way analogous to how Socrates (on the first interpretation of his dictum) seemed to be saying that those not engaging in self-examination would be better off not living?

This objection—that comparatively unintelligent people still have minds, albeit limited ones—is a fair challenge, to which Ryle owes us an answer. I suspect that he would reply that someone who is comparatively unintelligent in the sense, for instance, of achieving only a low percentile on standardized tests of mathematical or verbal ability, may still know how to construct a sentence, drive a car, or boil an egg. In that respect such a person can behave intelligently, even if he is less skilled in other activities than the majority of the population. On the other hand, if such an individual has lost his ability to do even these things, and is able to do nothing but breathe, metabolize food, and perform other automatic bodily functions, we would also be inclined to suggest that perhaps he is bereft of a mind after all. We do, note, use the term "vegetative state" to refer to someone who is only able to perform essential bodily functions, and this term suggests that such a person has the mental capacities that we associate with plants—namely, none at all.

One might also object to Ryle's position by pointing to the case of *"locked-in" syndrome*, also known as psuedocoma. A person afflicted with this syndrome is paralyzed across her entire body with the possible exception of being able to blink her eyes at will. (This extreme form of paralysis may result from of a variety of causes including stroke, severe spinal injury, and Lou Gehrig's Disease.) Nonetheless, such patients retain their cognitive function: they can still think, remember, feel emotions, and often retain proprioception, that is, an awareness of the positions of their limbs. (The "inner life" of such patients is powerfully depicted in the 2007 film, *The Butterfly and the Diving Bell*, directed by Julian Schnabel and based on a true story.) Patients with locked-in syndrome might seem to pose a challenge to Ryle's view, since they are able to think in spite of not being able to act. For if they cannot act, they cannot act intelligently either. So does Ryle have a chance of making sense of such cases, or do they spell the demise of his theory?

Ryle could reply to this challenge. However, one strategy for such a reply that might occur to you does not seem promising. This would be to say that even if a locked-in patient cannot act, and so cannot act intelligently, he is still disposed to do so. For perhaps he will someday recover and regain the full use of his body. Unfortunately, this defense of Ryle seems limited by the fact that some locked-in patients will, and in fact could, never recover from their affliction: they may have suffered neurological damage that is so severe as to be irreparable. But if that is the case, then trying to account for their intelligence by appealing to dispositions seems too much of a reach.

A more promising approach for Ryle would be to point out that a patient with locked-in syndrome is in fact able to act intelligently, even if her range of behavior is severely limited. After all, she can do such things as enumerate the prime numbers up to 200, remember the names of her high school teachers, or recite in her own thoughts a stanza of a poem by Rumi. She can also form images in her mind of past or imaginary events. Further, if she is starting to feel frustrated with her very difficult situation, she might make an effort to console herself by thinking positive thoughts, including remembering pleasant events from her own past and the people who participated in them. These activities might be hard or easy, she might plan to do one of them at a later date, and at such a later date she might even forget to do one of these things. In short, these activities bear all the hallmarks of action other than involving movements of muscles and limbs, while in no way suggesting that they're carried on in a non-physical realm.[2] What is more, Ryle could point out, the locked-in patient might at a certain moment be fast asleep and still be disposed to behave intelligently in this sense: for it could still be true that if she were to wake up, she would be able to recite poetry in the privacy of her thoughts, and likewise for the other activities we have just mentioned.

If this defense of Ryle is correct, then he would seem to have a genuine challenge to present to Descartes. For unless Descartes can make sense of a purely non-physical entity behaving intelligently, he will be unable to convince us that such an agent has a mind. And if that is the case, then we should doubt that it is even conceivable that one's mind could exist disembodied. Of course, we are all familiar with cartoon-style representations of angels, God, Satan, and the like. However, we have observed that these representations always portray such figures in physical form—as having wings, long beards, horns, cloven hooves, and so on, even though such representations sometimes also characterize their subjects as being partly ethereal. This is yet further reason to think that even with our best efforts, we are at a loss to conceive of purely non-physical minds.

Knowing Yourself through Extrospection

Descartes has a reasonably clear answer to the question how it is we know our minds: each of us is intimately connected to the contents of our minds via the properties of *infallibility* (if I think something is in my mind, then it is) and *phosphorescence* (if something is in my mind, then I am aware that it is). To appreciate why he holds these views, let us remind ourselves that we do seem to have a special authority on many aspects of our mentality:

> *Cognitive*: You tell yourself you believe that, for instance, air travel is safer than traveling by train or automobile. How could someone else convince you that you are wrong in ascribing that view to yourself? Notice that the only question at issue here is whether you do in fact *think* that air travel is safer than auto or train travel; we may set aside which of these modes of transportation really is the safest.

Affective: You believe you are feeling nervous because of the job interview that you have scheduled for tomorrow. You seem to be the final authority both on whether this feeling is one of nervousness, as well as a final authority on what the nervousness is about.

Experiential: You tell yourself that you are feeling a pain in your left leg, especially when you try to lift it while you are lying down. It is hard to see how anyone else could show that you are wrong in this belief.

Ryle will offer reasons to be skeptical about at least the first two of these three. At the same time, he owes an account of why, even if we are capable of being in error in such cases, we tend to be fairly reliable authorities on what is going on in our minds.

For the first issue, on how we can be wrong about the contents of our minds, take affective states first. If we can have emotions of which we are not aware, that would help make sense of why in other cases we mistakenly ascribe emotions to ourselves. Suppose for instance that you are jealous of Francesca for doing better than you did on this week's test in your history class. That jealousy might make it unpleasant for you to spend time with her. However, if it is difficult to acknowledge that jealousy, you might find yourself attributing the unpleasant feeling you experience in her presence to something else. Perhaps when she tries to chat with you, you feel uncomfortable but blame that feeling on the room's being too warm, or on the fact that other people a few tables away are talking too loudly, or on the color of the scarf she is wearing. Here would be a case of an emotion that you undergo but fail to recognize in full; but it still has consequences for how you experience your environment, and those consequences you might in turn explain by ascribing to yourself other feelings that you do not have.

It would also seem that one can be wrong about what cognitive state one is in. I might say to myself, "Airplane travel is perfectly safe!" On this basis, I conclude that I believe airplane travel to be perfectly safe. However, much of my other behavior suggests that I do not in fact believe this: I show signs of anxiety when I try to book airline tickets for an upcoming trip I need to take, I sweat and fidget while waiting at the gate for my flight, and when it comes time to board the plane, I can't seem to muster the courage to get on board. My actions, that is, suggest that I don't believe air travel to be safe in spite of what I've told myself.

With sufficient ingenuity we might even try to come up with cases in which one is wrong in one's view about what experiential state one is in. Lying in a hospital bed, I start to regain consciousness after a major operation. I feel pain in my left leg. Or so it seems: but I now remember that I just had a leg amputated, and the "pain" is in the limb that I just lost! How can I feel pain a limb that I no longer have? Some people might reply that I'm feeling pain alright, but I'm just mistaken about its location. Others might say that I only seem to feel pain, but am experiencing something else. Fortunately, we don't have to settle this dispute. Instead, it is enough to see that even the idea that we can't be mistaken about our experiential states, is not as self-evident as it might at first have seemed.

It seems, then, that we are not infallible about our affective and cognitive states. Perhaps we can even be mistaken about our experiential states, though this is a more controversial issue. For the second issue we mentioned above, of how we tend to be on the whole fairly well-informed about our state of mind, Ryle's answer is bracingly simple: we have this privileged access because we spend more time with ourselves than we do with other people! As in the title of John Kabat-Zinn's book, *Wherever You Go, There You Are*, so long as my head is attached to the rest of my body, I'll be able on the whole to keep track of my behavior. With some care I will also be able to keep track of my own dispositions to behavior, learning over time, for instance, that I tend to shy away from crowds and tend to pack too much clothing when I travel. These are things that another person could just as easily learn about me if they paid close enough attention. Similarly, are you wondering whether you're feeling shy at the social event you've just entered? Check to see if you've been sitting in the corner of the room absorbed in the antics of your host's cat. Wondering if you're partial to chocolate over strawberry ice cream? Place yourself in a position to choose between the two and see what happens.

From this vantage point, we can also see that for Ryle, privileged access marks a difference of degree rather than of kind, and is one that could in principle be reversed. Due to their position in my head, my eyes generally look away from my body rather than toward it. As result, if I am in the presence of another person over a long period, I might learn a great deal about her behavior and arrive at generalizations about her dispositions to behavior as well. We do, in fact, regularly keep tabs on other people, and in the course of doing so we learn whether they are fearful, irritated, elated, or hopeful. We also learn about more chronic aspects of their personalities such as whether they are empathetic, irascible, possessed of an off-color sense of humor or quick to take offense. What is more, if we are with a person for a very long period, such as occurs with couples who are together for many decades, it would come as no surprise to hear one pronounce authoritatively on what the other likes, dislikes, or believes. Could one member of a long-term relationship know better than the other what is in the other's mind?

Ryle would answer in the affirmative. In his chapter on self-knowledge in *The Concept of Mind*, for instance, he writes,

> A person's knowledge about himself and others may be distributed between many roughly distinguishable grades yielding correspondingly numerous roughly distinguishable senses of "knowledge." He may be aware that he is whistling "Tipperary" and not know that he is whistling it in order to give the appearance of a sang-froid which he does not feel. Or again, he may be aware that he is shamming sang-froid without knowing that the tremors he is trying to hide derive from the agitation of a guilty conscience.
>
> (1949, p. 180)

You may have found yourself whistling a tune in order to appear that you're feeling more carefree than you are in fact feeling. Perhaps you realized this later. But at the time, there was something that you were feeling—anxiety, perhaps—that you did not want to reveal, and did not even reveal to *yourself.* Even if such a thing has not happened to you, I am confident that you can think of others to whom it has happened. You might have thought to yourself: "George might think he's perfectly carefree in the presence of his old boyfriend, but that guy is clearly stirring up some unpleasant feelings in George, and that seems to be what the whistling is about." Here would be a case in which you feel you know George's mind better than he knows his own. In addition, you might conclude that if George thinks he knows his mind better than you do, because, after all, it is *his* mind, that wouldn't prove much. I don't know my weight better than the scale does simply because the body in question is my body and not the scale's! For the same reason I don't know my blood pressure better than does the blood pressure monitor. Why expect matters to be any different in the case of my mind?

Well, even if we would not *expect* matters to be different in the case of our minds, for experiential states and some aspects of affective states, matters do in fact seem to be different. Sometimes it is difficult to be sure whether the twinge I feel in my gut is hunger, nerves, or something else, but I can feel pretty sure I felt *something*. More dramatically, a high speed crash of the sort a cyclist could experience after hitting gravel on a steep descent might lacerate skin and break some bones. There is Svetlana on the side of the road after a bad spill, with bits of bicycle and flesh scattered around her. How could she possibly be wrong in judging herself to be in pain? So too, many emotions have a characteristic way that they feel. Strong anger feels one way, while strong happiness tends to feel another. While I may be in doubt about the cause of my happiness, it is very difficult to see how I could be mistaken in thinking I am feeling elation.

It seems doubtful that Ryle could acknowledge such phenomena while maintaining his low-key approach to self-knowledge. On Ryle's view, as we have seen, I know more about my own mind than I know about yours because I tend to spend more time with myself than I do with you. Such asymmetry as there may be between my knowledge of my own mind and my knowledge of yours is a difference of degree only, and is in principle one that could be reversed if I were to spend enough time with you. Yet my knowledge of my experiential states, such as pain, and my knowledge of the qualitative dimension of emotions, when these occur, seem too robust to fit within Ryle's framework. Let's see why.

Thinking Embodied

It might seem that by challenging Descartes' argument for his dualistic conclusion, Ryle would naturally advocate a materialist monist position to be put in its place. However, Ryle also abjures that metaphysical view. His reason for doing so is that according to his way of thinking, both materialism and dualism are answers to a confused question. That question is, what kind of substance is a mind—material or non-material? As you can now appreciate, Ryle will deny that the mind is any kind of substance at all. Rather, insofar as we want to ask about minds, we should ask what it is to be intelligent, and *that* question, Ryle urges, should in turn be replaced with the question, what is it to behave, or to be disposed to behave, intelligently.

The opposition between materialist monism and dualism cannot be brushed aside quite so easily, however. Recall that for Ryle, minds are clusters of multi-track dispositions toward intelligent behavior. Two further questions beyond those we have already addressed may be raised about his approach. One of these questions is whether all mental phenomena can be accurately captured in dispositional terms. The other asks, even if all mental phenomena can be so captured, whether it is true that we can avoid questions of materialism versus dualism. Concerning the first question: perhaps it is true that a person who believes it is about to rain will be disposed to act in certain ways: grabbing an umbrella or coat, making sure that her windows are closed, choosing to take a bus rather than a bike to work, and so forth. Can we expect a similar approach to experiential states to be plausible? No doubt, someone who is in pain is disposed to wince, cry out with an "Ouch!" and move away from whatever might be the source of the pain, such as the jagged piece of glass she has just scraped against. But it is difficult to see how this dispositional account will capture what it is for pain to feel the way that it does.

To appreciate the problem, consider two distinct but unpleasant smells, such as the rotten-egg smell of sulfur, and the smell of a skunk. (If you have yet to experience both of these smells, just reformulate the example with two unpleasant, but distinct experiences, that you can remember having.) Those two are certainly different smells; I could tell them apart blindfolded. And so the olfactory experience of sulfur is different from the olfactory experience of skunk. That is, these experiences are two different mental states or processes. Ryle's view will imply that these two different mental states will be associated with different dispositions to behavior. But is that so? Either such state will dispose me to say things like "Yuk!" and perhaps hold my nose. I will try to move away from the source of the odor. Perhaps I will seek out a more pleasant odor to mask the one I am now experiencing. But notice that these dispositions to behavior are the same for the two olfactory experiences. It would seem to follow that Ryle is committed to holding that these are not "two" experiences after all, but one. More precisely, Ryle seems to be committed to holding that just as a sulfur smell at noon is an experience of the same type as another sulfur smell at 1 pm, so too, he would seem to have to say that a sulfur smell at noon is an experience of the same type as a skunk smell at 1 pm. But that seems to fly in the face of our experiences, which show us that a sulfur smell is a different experience from a skunk smell.

Someone might reply on Ryle's behalf that the behavioral dispositions differentiating the two experiences are distinct because they dispose us to different types of *verbal* behavior. For one of those experience will tend to make us say, "Sulfur, yuk!" while another will make us say, "Skunk, eew!" or some such thing. This may be true for those people who are in the habit of naming their experience. Observe, though, that someone would be able to note the difference between these two experiences even if he did not have words that we could use to differentiate them. So too, I am confident that you can differentiate between the smell of two spices, for instance, even if you do not know what they are called. Accordingly, appealing to language as a way of distinguishing the dispositions associated with the sulfur and the skunk smells does not appear to be a promising route to defending Ryle.

Ryle, then, seems to have a gap in his theory on the issue of differentiating in behavioral terms between certain pairs of experiences that seem quite different. However, his theory faces a broader challenge on the issue of completeness. To appreciate the issue, note that as scientific understanding progresses, we often discover why certain dispositions have the features that they do. Further, we tend to do that by elucidating the physical basis of those dispositions. It is true that salt dissolves in unsaturated liquid such as water. However, we might want to know why it does so, and physical chemistry tells us why in terms of the molecular structure of salt on the one hand and water on the other. Similarly, everyday experience tells us that walking around in socks on a carpet in dry weather is likely to produce some static electricity. Physics tells us why this is so, and its discovery of the explanation a few centuries ago was a major intellectual advance. But then, should we not also expect a similar account of the basis of our dispositions to intelligent behavior?

This is the crux of a challenge to Ryle that was posed in the 1960s by the philosopher David Armstrong (1968). Sure, he would say, when someone is angry they're disposed to use colorful language, throw things, scowl, clench their fists, and the like. However, we might want to know *why* it is that anger disposes us to behave in these ways. Armstrong proposes that perhaps the explanation lies in the properties of our central nervous system (CNS). Just as properties of our CNS explain why under certain conditions a person becomes forgetful or anxious, we might expect that other properties of the CNS account for why an emotion such as anger disposes us to behave in one characteristic set of ways, while an emotion such as, for instance, fear, disposes us to behave in a distinct, yet still characteristic, set of ways.

Armstrong goes on to propose a materialistic position which, you will recall, holds that minds (or mental processes) are purely physical. This in turn suggests that cognitive, affective, and experiential states or processes are all physical as well. In so doing, Armstrong can agree with Ryle that such mental states and processes are intimately bound up with dispositions to behavior, but he may also point out that we have only done some of our explanatory work by noting this. We also need to dig deeper and look into why this is so.

By adopting this materialist position, Armstrong is still on firmer ground than his predecessors such as Thomas Hobbes or Julian Offray de La Mettrie. For he can stand on Ryle's shoulders and point out that insofar as mentality is crucially linked up with dispositions toward intelligent behavior, we may still see where Descartes' argument for dualism goes wrong. A disembodied entity (were such a thing to exist) could not behave intelligently, and so could not be minded. At the same time, Armstrong could point to neuroscience as a source of explanation of why various mental states produce the behaviors that they do.

It will, however, be a considerably greater challenge to appeal to neuroscience to explain experiential states. It is difficult to see how to account for an experience such as the smell of sulfur or the visual appearance of something red, in terms of goings on in our central nervous system. Such an account would, one would think, explain on the basis of what is occurring in the brain, why the experience has the features that it does. One such cerebral event should account for why the smell of sulfur has the character it does, while another such event should account for why the smell of skunk has the character that *it* does. However, current scientific knowledge does not provide such insight.

Notwithstanding this lacuna in Armstrong's (and in any other materialist monist's) theory, he also offers a bracingly straightforward account of our ability to know our own minds that is an alternative to both Ryle's and Descartes' approach. For Armstrong, the minds of higher-level creatures (including but not necessarily limited to our own species) are equipped with internal "scanners" whose job it is to keep track of what is going within them. Just as a robot might be able to track its own level of battery power and modify its behavior when it is running low, so too an internal scanner of the sort that Armstrong posits can detect when the mind it is scanning is in a state of fear, hunger, surprise, or enthusiasm, and redirect the organism's behavior accordingly. In offering such a hypothesis, Armstrong is not suggesting that each of us has a homunculus, or intelligent smaller person, within them. (Explanations of intelligence in terms of homunculi are notoriously unsatisfactory, since they merely raise the question: how do you explain the homunculus' intelligence?) Rather, Armstrong is positing a mechanism that is sophisticated enough to detect things going on within the organism, and that need not itself be a mind. We also need not assume that such an inner scanner always operates perfectly, since any given mechanism within us can be expected to go awry sooner or later. On the other hand, Armstrong's account of self-knowledge seems ill-equipped to explain why our failures of self-awareness at times seem so persistent, so willful, and on occasion downright perverse. In the next chapter we will direct our attention to this last theme.

Chapter Summary

- Behaviorism comes in a number of varieties, and that associated with Gilbert Ryle is in some respects more sophisticated than that associated with behaviorist movement in academic psychology in the early to middle years of the twentieth century.
- Ryle construes the mind as a set of multi-track dispositions to intelligent behavior.
- Supporting this construal is a distinction between knowing how (what we previously termed propositional knowledge) and knowing that (ability knowledge).

- Ryle charges Descartes with committing a category mistake in supposing that a mind could exist entirely disembodied. Such an alleged mind would be unable to act intelligently.
- Ryle also offers a conception of self-knowledge focusing on extrospection rather than introspection.
- Although he rejects both dualism and materialism on the grounds that they are answers to a confused question, Armstrong argues that Ryle cannot avoid addressing that question.
- Armstrong offers, as a refinement of Ryle's view, a materialistic monism that also suggests an account of our knowledge of our own minds.

Study Questions

1. Consider the list we discussed above (being a good bird spotter, having a refined fashion sense, being a whiz at quadratic equations, being an excellent judge of horses, having perfect pitch) of forms of intelligence. Next, choose two items from this list and show how they may be analyzed in dispositional terms.
2. Please explain Ryle's distinction between propositional and ability knowledge. Can either form of knowledge be directed toward oneself? Please explain your answer.
3. Given Ryle's view of what it is to have a mind, might non-human animals have minds? Please explain your answer.
4. What are Ryle's reasons for denying that it is even in principle possible for there to be a disembodied mind?
5. Ryle contends that one's knowledge of one's mind differs in degree, rather than in kind, from one's knowledge of the minds of others. Please explain his reasons for this view.
6. Ryle uses the example of a man whistling Tipperary to illustrate some of the ways in which we might deceive ourselves. Please formulate your own example of a behavior or set of behaviors by means of which a person might deceive herself.
7. We raised an objection to Ryle's account of experiential states with the help of an example involving the smells of sulfur and of skunk. Please formulate an analogous example involving a different sensory modality such as vision, sound, touch, or taste.
8. Ryle rejects both materialistic monism and dualism. Please explain his reasons for doing so.
9. How does Armstrong criticize Ryle's refusal to take sides between the dualist and materialist views of the mind?

Notes

1. The song, "I'll Fly Away," by Allison Krauss and Gillian Welch, for instance, contains lyrics suggesting that after the body is destroyed, there will continue to be a self that survives that event: "Some bright morning when this life is over—I'll fly away—To that home on God's celestial shore—I'll fly away."

2. Neuroscientists have of late been able to measure the effort locked-in patients exert in such activities with devices including fMRI machines. See for instance R. deCharms (2008) "Applications of Real-Time fMRI," *Nature Reviews Neuroscience*, vol. 9, pp. 720–9.

Introductory Further Readings

Armstrong, D. (1968) *A Materialist Theory of Mind*, Revised Edition (New York: Routledge). Classic and detailed exposition and defense of materialism, including influential criticisms of Ryle.

Heil, J. (2004) *Philosophy of Mind: A Contemporary Introduction* (New York and London: Routledge). Accessible introduction to general issues in philosophy of mind.

Lowe, E. J. (2000) *An Introduction to the Philosophy of Mind* (Cambridge: Cambridge University Press). Accessible introduction to the main issues in contemporary philosophy of mind.

Ravenscroft, I. (2005) *Philosophy of Mind: A Beginner's Guide* (Oxford: Oxford University Press. Overview of the field written specifically for those new to philosophy.

Ryle, G. (1949) *The Concept of Mind*, (Chicago: University of Chicago Press). Classic work defending a form of behaviorism while providing a sustained critique of dualism.

Advanced Further Readings

Chalmers, D. (2002) *Philosophy of Mind: Classical and Contemporary Readings* (Oxford: Oxford University Press). Massive anthology with impressive coverage of this large field.

Lycan, W. (1996) *Consciousness and Experience* (Cambridge, MA: MIT Press). Inspired by Armstrong, a sophisticated defense of the "higher order thought" theory of consciousness.

Moffett, M. (2014) *Knowing How: Essays on Knowledge, Mind and Action* (Oxford: Oxford University Press). State of the art essays on the significance of the distinction between propositional and ability knowledge.

Internet Resources

Tanney, J. (2015) 'Gilbert Ryle,' in *The Stanford Encyclopedia of Philosophy* (https://plato.stanford.edu/entries/ryle/). Insightful overview of Ryle's contribution of philosophy.

4   The Freudian Unconscious

Introduction

This chapter introduces psychoanalysis, whose influence during the last century is now easy to underestimate as a result of its waning prestige. I introduce psychoanalysis by discussing a work of its most influential exponent, Sigmund Freud's *Introductory Lectures on Psychoanalysis* (ILP). There Freud motivates aspects of his approach by reference to what he calls parapraxes (which have since then come to be called Freudian slips). This is an entertaining topic of which we all have personal experience. At the same time it allows us to introduce the notion of the unconscious, but I am at pains to highlight ambiguities in the notion as well as the different uses to which it is put by Freud and others. In addition, we need to be wary of the epistemological shell game that defenders of psychoanalysis sometimes engage in, such as accusing anyone challenging their theory of suffering from "resistance." We illustrate the dangers here with reference to the psychoanalytic account of dream symbolism, concluding that while psychoanalysis offers a fascinating theory of much human behavior, it is in need of experimental validation. The chapter closes with a brief discussion of what such a validation might look like.

Slips of the Tongue and Other Minutiae

Over the last several decades it has become part of common sense that some of what we do is the result of emotions and other attitudes of which we are not aware. Demetrius is being homophobic, and we suspect that his attitude toward LGBTQ people stems from repressed homosexual urges that he is blind to. Suleika is being passive-aggressive, and that is why she is not answering our messages even though she is unaware that this is the reason for her behavior. Most of us are familiar with the idea that some portion of the mind is outside of awareness, and that that portion contains desires, fears, and other attitudes that might be unpleasant or even painful to acknowledge as being within us. However, before the final decades of the nineteenth century, such claims would have been rejected by most people as ludicrous. To such people, the idea that one's mind might contain material of which one is unaware would have seemed nearly a contradiction in terms. (Just think of how Descartes' project of rebuilding the sciences from unquestionable foundations depends, as we saw in Chapter 2, on our being able to know with absolute certainty what is in our own minds.) How did we get to where we are today, and do we have good reasons for staying here?

In this chapter I will focus on Sigmund Freud's classic, *Introductory Lectures on Psychoanalysis*, which is the transcript of lectures that he delivered in Vienna between 1916 and 1917. Freud published many other volumes, some even more famous than this one, but I've found this text to be ideal for introducing students to the flavor of his thought without our getting bogged down in details that needlessly detract from the central themes. The work is also useful for displaying both the explanatory power of Freud's new theory as well as its limitations. Recall that Socrates, before being sentenced to death by his fellow Athenians for allegedly corrupting the youth of that city, remarked that he thinks of himself as a gadfly whose job was to provoke the noble steed that is Athens into greater self-awareness. Over two millennia later, Freud was no less provocative, and to a much larger audience than Socrates had at his disposal. How did Freud manage to do this?

Let us start with the idea of the unconscious. I've heard it said that the unconscious is by definition unknowable. After all, one might suggest, it is part of the definition of the unconscious that you can't know your unconscious thoughts by introspecting. So, one might continue, while the unconscious may be real, it's beyond the reach of knowledge, and of science more generally. Unfortunately, this line of reasoning harbors two confusions. First of all, as we will see shortly, only some unconscious phenomena are absolutely beyond the scope of introspection. Other unconscious phenomena are open to introspection with some effort, even if they are not immediately evident upon our first glance within. Second, it is not the case that the only way to know about an unconscious phenomenon within me is by introspection. Perhaps I can know about unconscious phenomena occurring inside my mind in some way other than introspection. But what might that way be?

As we approach an answer to this question, it helps first to note that Freud mixes some quite reasonable ideas with others that are dubious. The dubious ideas include not only hypotheses that are not well supported by the data, but also views about what would count as sufficient evidence for, or a potential challenge to, his theory. These views enable Freud to practice what I shall call *epistemic hijinks*, that is, a kind of intellectual shell-game that would enable its practitioner to "prove" nearly any theory—about astrology, witchcraft, extra-sensory perception—take your pick. We will return later in this chapter to explain further what this hijinks is all about. For now, however, let's observe that in answer to the question how I might know about unconscious mental events, Freud makes a novel suggestion. There may be aspects of my own *behavior* that are best accounted for by supposing that they have unconscious causes. Such behavior is knowable not by introspection, but rather in a way I could use to learn about anyone else's behavior, namely, in a "third-personal" way. Just as I can hear you talking, I can hear myself doing so, and if there is a mirror handy, I can even watch my own behavior just as I can watch yours. Freud's initial conjecture about the value of taking a third-personal approach to one's own behavior concerns what he calls *parapraxes*: slips of the tongue, misplacing objects, forgetting things, and other seemingly trivial, everyday errors. For instance, you keep on misplacing a piece of jewelry that someone gave you as a gift; or in your job as a server in a restaurant you've caught yourself more than once bringing the bill to the male at the table rather than to the female diner with no prior indication of who was supposed to pay.

Freud gives many similar examples, including one in which a speaker proposing a toast on a ceremonial occasion calls on his audience to hiccough to (*aufstossen*) the health of the Chief, whereas he presumably intended to ask his audience to toast (*anstossen*) the health of the Chief (ILP, pp. 59–60). Freud also cites an historical case in which the president of Germany's Lower House of Parliament once opened proceedings with words that translate into English as, "Gentlemen, I take notice that a full quorum of members is present and herewith declare the sitting *closed*," when he had intended to declare the proceedings open. Similarly, an internet search with terms such as "Hilarious Freudian slips on the news" will deliver many hours of amusing clips in which newscasters and other public figures tripped over their words with quite embarrassing results, such as a famous case in which Mayor Richard J. Daley of Chicago remarks, "A policeman isn't there to create disorder. A policeman is there to preserve disorder."

Freud's parapraxes are now, of course, called Freudian slips, and it is part of contemporary common sense to explain someone's behavior in terms of this concept: the idea here is that the behavior was not just a mistake, but had a source that is itself psychological and yet not readily available to introspection.[1] For instance, perhaps you persisted in forgetting to respond to a message from your old friend because something about the prospect of re-establishing contact with him seemed unsavory: maybe you fear that doing so will reactivate your resentment toward him for prevailing in a competitive situation that occurred long ago, or some part of you now feels that he is not the kind of person you want to be associating with any longer. In the cases that Freud offers, perhaps the speaker proposing a toast to the Chief was unknowingly ambivalent toward his boss. Similarly, maybe the president of the Lower House was anxious, without being aware of it, about the business that Parliament had to conduct that day, and his words betrayed that anxiety. And just possibly Mayor Richard J. Daley harbored, without knowing it, some unsavory ideas for what the Chicago Police should be doing with their time.

Such explanations, Freud will urge, are no different in principle from others we offer in the sciences. The theory of plate tectonics, for instance, was developed at about the same time Freud was giving his introductory lectures on psychoanalysis, and it proposed to account for earthquakes, continental drift, and the creation of mountains and oceanic ridges and trenches. The theory was not accepted by the scientific community for another four decades, but its acceptance was driven by a basic principle known as

> *Inference to the Best Explanation* (IBE): given a range of otherwise puzzling phenomena, the best explanation to account for that phenomena is one that we are justified in accepting.

What counts as "best" here? Presumably the best explanation of a range of phenomena will be one that is internally coherent rather than self-contradictory, externally coherent in the sense of being consistent with other theories that are already established, and simpler than the other accounts of the phenomena that are available. To get a feel for this notion of simplicity, consider the old dictum, "When you hear hoof beats, think horses, not zebras." The suggestion behind the dictum is that while zebras *might* be responsible for the sound we're hearing, most of us live in environments in which horses are more plentiful than zebras. As a result, the zebra-based explanation of the phenomenon for which we seek an account is internally and externally coherent, but requires a complex set of hypotheses about how zebras might have made their way to, say, a forest outside Helsinki or a park in downtown Seoul (depending on where we are). A simpler theory is that horses made the hoof beats. More broadly, many advances in science over the millennia in which our species have been speculating about the causes behind observable events, have come from someone's offering an explanation that is simpler than that commonly accepted at the time, while being both internally and externally coherent.

Freud is in effect suggesting that parapraxes can be accounted for with a similar strategy. We start with a pattern of observable behavior (misplacing an object, delivering bills to male rather than female diners, etc.) and then ask, what would best explain such behavior? Knowing that simplicity is a virtue in any theory, in the sense that all else being equal, the simpler our account of a phenomenon, the better, Freud first considers the idea that these everyday mistakes are mere errors with no particularly interesting psychological cause. After all, sometimes we just do trip on the edge of a rug, break a glass, put a slip of paper in the wrong person's hand, and make other kinds of performance goofs. Freud will reply that this style of explanation will not account for *patterns* of error; perhaps tripping on the rug's edge is a one-off case, yet I *keep on* misplacing that toe-ring you gave me; you deliver checks to male diners *more often than not over a long period of time*, and yet another person *continues* to call you by the wrong name. Such patterns in behavior (which, remember, are all available to third-personal observation) call out for an explanation going deeper than the mere fact that we occasionally make mistakes.

Here is where Freud will posit *psychological causes of which we are not aware*. These are not the same as *causes* of which we are not aware. A single case of stepping on your little brother's homework might be due to its being where it should not have been; at least when you stepped on it, you were not aware of its location on the living room floor, and there is no reason why you should have been. On the other hand, Freud suggests, a pattern of mistakes is better explained by something having a more general reach, a prime example of which would be, for instance, a feeling of animosity toward your sibling. Such animosity might take the form of jealousy, resentment, or anger, but what matters for us now is that animosity is always a psychological phenomenon and, at least until it is satisfied or otherwise relieved, will keep affecting what you do. Fear might be of a particular thing, such as the enraged dog rushing toward me. On the other hand, fear may also be about a class of things, such as spiders, heights, or closed spaces that one cannot leave at will. This is why, even if a person honestly and in good faith has no awareness of feeling fearful of such closed spaces, she might nevertheless continually avoid subways and airplanes, and show a strong aversion to spelunking. It might take some painstaking work to figure out what underlies this pattern of behavior.

Freud will call such mental states of which we are unaware unconscious, thereby contrasting them with those that are conscious. Suppose you are figuring out how to get to a job interview next week at an appointed time. This might require some careful planning: "I'll need to take the #4 tram from 14th to 38th street, then walk three blocks to the building at the address I was given. But if it's raining I should take a cab or have an umbrella handy." This planning is a relatively deliberate and effortful act of the mind, and when you think, "I'll need to take the #4 tram from 14th to 38th Street," that thought is probably conscious: you not only think that thought, you may easily notice yourself doing so. Similarly when you find yourself feeling angry about being cut off by another pedestrian as you walk to work, the feeling is most likely a conscious experience. But, Freud is now suggesting, there is nothing in the nature of a mental state requiring it to be conscious. That is, you can undergo a cognitive or affective state without being aware of the fact that you are doing so. (It is less clear that this is possible for an experiential state.)

Two Ways of Being Unconscious

Before we proceed further into a discussion of the unconscious, it will be helpful to distinguish it from the more inclusive category of events that are nonconscious, as well as to distinguish the unconscious into two categories. First of all, just because an event—even one that is going on inside me—is nonconscious, does not mean it is in any sense mental. When my liver removes toxins from my bloodstream, when cells divide in my body, and when antibodies fight bacteria, these are all events within me that are non-conscious. This is simply because it is not the case that they are conscious events. But none of them is in any sense mental: after all, they are not cognitive events (like believing that my liver is functioning well), or affective events (like feeling elated about cell division), or experiential events (like savoring the taste of a papaya or taking in the aroma of a carob tree in bloom), though of course they might result in bodily changes that could in turn bring about such events. (For instance, if leukocytes within my body fail to triumph against bacteria, I will likely fall ill, much to my chagrin.) As you can see, the vast majority of events, from stars colliding to cells dividing, are non-conscious and indeed non-mental. By contrast, to be *unconscious*, an event must be not only non-conscious, but also mental. This means that if there are any unconscious events, they will have to be either cognitive, affective, or experiential events that I can undergo without being aware of in a first-personal way.

I have tried to make a case on Freud's behalf that the very idea of an unconscious event is not incoherent, since there seems to be nothing in the nature of a mental event requiring that I be conscious of it just by virtue of its occurring within me. But plenty of coherent concepts seem not to have any instances in nature: I could define a "flimp" as a three-headed reptile, without thereby expecting to find any such creatures in nature. Perhaps unconscious phenomena are like flimps: an intelligible concept but without any instances in reality. On the other hand, we may now notice that Freud is suggesting that the best explanation of a range or pattern of behavior that would otherwise be mysterious is that such behavior results from unconscious phenomena. Chance forgetting might account for why once or twice you forgot to respond to that message from your old friend. However, chance forgetting seems a less plausible account of why you have such a persistent pattern of forgetting to reply. It seems quite unlikely that for the past seven months you simply *happened* to forget to respond to your old friend's message, particularly given how much time you've spent during that period on social media!

So too, Freud would suggest, for the president of the Lower House. Some slips of the tongue may be due to the fact that certain pairs of words are pronounced similarly. However, the German for "open" (*öffnen*) and "closed" (*abgeschlossen*) are not very similar. For this reason, the observation that our tongue and lips don't always behave as we want them to do, seems inadequate to account for the president's saying *abgeschlossen* rather than any of a large number of words more similar to *öffnen*. Instead, Freud hypothesizes that the president may unconsciously have desired to avoid the discussion slated for that day, and that this desire compelled his mouth to help him achieve its aim by declaring the proceedings closed.

Freud, then, is suggesting that some of our behavior is best explained on the hypothesis that it is caused by unconscious phenomena. Part of his reason for this position is that is that it enables Freud to say that an explanation in terms of the unconscious is, at least in this case, preferable to others due to its relative simplicity. Just as scientists might hypothesize entities that may at first seem mysterious but that end up, over time, making sense of a considerable range of puzzling phenomena, so too, we may overcome our hostility toward unconscious causes of our behavior once we see what a wide range of behavior begins to make sense in its light.

Positing the unconscious may, then, do some explanatory work. To give such a posit a fighting chance of success, we do well to draw a further distinction. That is a distinction within the unconscious between the *pre-conscious* and *subconscious*. An unconscious event is pre-conscious just in case it is unconscious but capable of being made conscious with sufficient effort. By contrast, a sub-conscious event is one that is unconscious and not capable of being made conscious even with one's best effort to make it so. To illustrate the first notion, consider that right now you probably know the names of many more people than you can recollect at this moment: childhood friends, elementary school teachers, first romantic interests, musical groups you once admired, or cities you've visited. With some time and effort, you can probably bring to mind many of these names. But when you do so, you are not *learning* anything new. This suggests that before you recollected them, you knew these names even if that knowledge was not conscious. However, because knowledge is a mental, and more specifically a cognitive phenomenon, what you brought into consciousness was not just non-conscious like metabolism, but was more specifically unconscious. And what is more, since you were able to bring up this knowledge to consciousness with some effort, that knowledge was not just unconscious, but also pre-conscious.

Notice an implication of this notion of the pre-conscious. Once you know about a pre-conscious item in a first-personal way, it is no longer unconscious but has made its way into the conscious part of your mind. This is as it should be from the point of view of Freud's theory of the unconscious. At the same time, you might have good reason to suppose that you have pre-conscious items inside you, but that good reason might be entirely of a "third-personal" variety. In that case, you might know about these unconscious items without thereby pushing them across the conscious/non-conscious boundary.

The posit of *sub*conscious phenomena is, as you might imagine, more ambitious and also more controversial than is a posit of the pre-conscious. We will return to the evidence for such phenomena in the next chapter. At least in ILP, however, Freud's view seems to be that all unconscious phenomena are pre-conscious. With enough effort, and most likely with the aid of long hours in talk-therapy, you can bring up into conscious awareness those feelings that cause your parapraxes. Coming to grips with such feelings may be painful and even shocking, but Freud holds it can always be done. Further, I would venture that you may have experienced just such a "surfacing": try to bring yourself back to the rage and humiliation that you felt as a child when that classmate embarrassed you in front of other kids—or substitute some other childhood experience that reignites some long-ago drama. Roll it around in your mind a little; put yourself back in that space. I would predict that after not too long, you will find that that feeling has not altogether disappeared, but has been in some sense inside of you for all these years. If Freud is right, it was, until a moment ago, an unconscious, and more precisely a pre-conscious emotion.

Functions of the Unconscious Mind

At this point it would be reasonable to ask, even if positing unconscious, and more specifically pre-conscious phenomena is coherent, and supported by some empirical evidence, why should the human (or for that matter, any other species') mind contain unconscious items? What, if anything, is accomplished by storing mental material outside of conscious awareness? Freud gives a fascinating answer to this question, and we will see in the next chapter a very different answer that more recent research has offered.

Freud starts with a hypothesis about human nature: in the absence of any culture or other civilizing force to rein them in, we are creatures of our impulses, and aside from those fulfilling immediate bodily needs such as hunger and thirst, those impulses are more often than not of a violent and sexual nature. Without any authority such as law enforcement or the threat of embarrassment among our peers, we will, Freud says, attack another person if he has something that we want. And without any such authority, Freud says, we are apt to act on our sexual desires by attempting to have intercourse with the first available target. As a result, if we can get away with it, we will rape whenever the urge for sex possesses us, and steal whenever the desire for something that someone else has comes along. If doing either of these things requires inflicting harm on another person, then, this line of thought goes, that is just too bad for them.

Many works of fiction portray how things might be if human nature as Freud conceives it were to have free rein: Stanley Kubrick's *A Clockwork Orange*, and the more recent movie, *The Purge* (directed by James DeMonaco) are just a few examples. In the former, the psychopathic delinquent Alex Delarge and his gang rampage through a future Britain, indulging all their urges toward sexuality and violence. In the latter, we are asked to imagine a society in which for a 12-hour period each year, no activity is illegal. During that period, as one might expect, urges toward sexuality and violence are given free reign.

Well, you might ask, in a world (fictional or otherwise) in which people's sexual and violent urges are not constrained, would not chaos reign, with the likely consequence that we would wipe ourselves out after a while? Freud would reply, I suspect, that this probably would happen, and may be what *did* happen first, to species of hominids other than *Homo sapiens*. That, he might suggest, could account why those species have become extinct. Second, groups of people from our own species' past may well have lived in just such a licentious way, and perhaps that is why relatively short-lived societies tend to be the norm in the history (and pre-history) of our species.

More positively, Freud might suggest that the need to avoid the mayhem that would result from our acting on our instincts is precisely the, or, at least, an important role of social norms, of which laws are a special case. Laws, at least when enforced with enough vigor to make people fear imprisonment, torture, or even death if caught, may deter people from acting on their natural impulses. In addition, and at least as important, many social norms that are not formulated as laws may still regulate behavior: you will likely feel embarrassed if you are caught doing something that your social group frowns upon even if getting caught does not result in imprisonment or some other legal sanction. And that threat of embarrassment may well deter you from acting on an impulse.

The suggestion here, then, is that human nature is inherently prone to unfettered sexuality and violence. Further, if such impulses are left to their own devices, we are in danger of wiping ourselves out, or if not, then at least living quite unpleasant lives. This is a problem to which social norms are potential solutions. At least a good portion of people will learn to respect other people's property if they know that not doing so will get them in huge trouble, and at least most people will learn to refrain from trying to rape the first person they see whom they find sexually appealing. Of course, even with social norms in force, some people will still not learn to control themselves, and I suspect that Freud will say that this is why prisons and other institutions of incarceration will not be going out of business any time soon.

None of the above is to say that some early Eritrean or Mesopotamian ruler presciently grasped Freud's theory and began to institute social norms in order to preserve social stability. That is a possible, but not a necessary part of Freud's theory. Rather, social norms can come into play without anyone's intending them to do so. Have you ever noticed that when you are having a face-to-face conversation with someone, you start to talk slightly before they finish their sentence? This is a well-established phenomenon in linguistics,[2] and it is not considered rude to start speaking over someone as long as you don't begin your intervention too early. But we do well to doubt that any conversation czar ever decreed that henceforth it will be permissible to begin speaking slightly before your conversation partner is done speaking! Instead, this practice may have just been stumbled upon as a happy accident, and then made those conversations using it more efficient than those that did not. This may have been how it caught on.

So too, the idea of personal property that others cannot confiscate just because they want some of it for themselves, might have been instituted by an explicit decree, and by an authority figure whose aim was to make social life run more smoothly. But it need not have been that way. Instead, the institution of personal property might have taken shape in the implicit, and possibly accidental way that most likely occurred in the development of conversational turn-taking. Freud's theory doesn't have to take a stand on this issue, just as he need not take a stand on the issue of how most of us came to keep most of our sexual impulses in check.

Even if social norms teach us to keep our impulses in check, impulses toward sexuality and violence are not the kinds of thing that we can simply scrub away with sufficient determination. Instead, those impulses will still be within us, but not consciously. That is, for Freud, the unconscious is a repository for psychic material that is suppressed in the interest of smooth functioning of society. If that material were conscious, we would be all too prone to act on it. Instead, and given that we cannot simply eradicate these impulses, a second-best solution is to push these impulses into the unconscious part of our minds.

Freud's theory does predict that in those situations in which social norms become frayed, human impulses toward sexuality and violence tend to surface. Recall that the lectures that formed the basis of ILP were given in the final years of World War I. Freud lived to see the onset of World War II as well, and as a result of these experiences would likely have said that these events provide ample source material for understanding the breakdown of social norms and the forms of behavior that result. So too, he could point to many other periods in human history in which human impulses particularly to violence were given free rein, and the mayhem that resulted.

We can't scrub away our impulses to sexuality and violence. However, one might be tempted to suggest that so long as social norms encourage us to keep these impulses bottled up inside, all will be well. Freud will even be doubtful of this idea, which conjures a society of Puritans who rigidly adhere to the norms of polite behavior but never permit themselves to blow off steam. His reason for being doubtful is that the suppression of our impulses is always an unstable solution to the problem that their existence presents. No matter how hard we try to keep those impulses locked up inside, they have a funny way of bubbling up to the surface, often with disturbing results. Perhaps Freud would suggest that the witch hunts that Puritans engaged in were the result of just such a bubbling up. Is there an alternative in which we might give limited expression to our impulses without burning alleged witches or otherwise causing others undue suffering? For Freud, this is one role for activities in which we get partial and often vicarious satisfaction of our impulses, such as sports, either engaged in or enjoyed by spectators. It is not too far-fetched to see spectators of American football, as they scream their lungs out in front of players smashing into one another on their television screens, as getting satisfaction, on some level, of their own impulses toward violence. Similar remarks apply to rugby, Mixed Martial Arts, and other more violent sports. Add violent video games, horror movies, splatterpunk fiction, and the musical genre of death metal, and you have an impressive array of options for partial fulfillment of one's impulses toward violence.[3] Freud terms this process of partial fulfillment of our unconscious desires by other means, *sublimation.*

Of course, we need some real, and not just virtual, ways of satisfying our sexual impulses, since otherwise our species will perish. Perhaps institutions such as marriage are one means of fulfilling those impulses in a way that keeps the species going, but that also keeps us from allowing our sexual impulses from taking over. (Remember that monogamy is only one form of marriage institution; societies with polygamy would also limit sexual impulses, but provide a wider space in which to fulfill them than does monogamy.) At the same time, many societies do have practices that one may reasonably conjecture enable the vicarious fulfillment of our sexual desires. Dancing is one such case. You may also find it useful to consider whether some of the pleasure we take in food goes beyond its nutritional value and flavor: it may be that when we enjoy the texture of a certain kind of food, that enjoyment stems from our receiving vicarious satisfaction of our sexual impulses. We need not here settle whether this conjecture is true, but one may wonder how much of our interaction with food is driven by our sexual appetites and not just caloric needs.

Explaining Dreams

Freud views dreams, when properly understood, as windows into the unconscious. His account of dreams starts with the suggestion that the primary function of sleep is for bodily regeneration (ILP, p. 108). Freud further contends that a dreamless sleep is the best kind since it allows the body to regenerate itself most efficiently. However, Freud tells us, sometimes while sleeping we might experience a distraction stemming from either an external or an internal source. An external distraction might be an alarm clock: it rings away, threatening to interrupt our peaceful slumber. An internal source might be a bodily need such as hunger, an impulse to urinate, or sexual arousal. Responding to the alarm clock, say by turning it off, threatens to wake us up, and of course eating or going to the bathroom to urinate requires getting out of bed.

How might our mind respond to such threats to continued sleep in such a way as to protect it? Freud writes, "A dream . . . is the manner in which the mind reacts to stimuli that impinge upon it in the state of sleep." (ILP, p. 109) In a later chapter he elaborates, remarking in particular that dreams do this by means of hallucinatory satisfaction of our desires (ILP, p. 167). To appreciate Freud's hypothesis, think of a typical daydream: you are hard at work in your cubicle on a freezing and blustery Tuesday morning, but as you analyze a contract or study a building plan, you imagine yourself floating down a gently winding river on a warm afternoon with a cool drink in your hand and a number of friends floating alongside you. Or you daydream that you are in front-row seats at a music festival screaming your lungs out as the Alpaca Lips (who else?!) jam away. Then your boss passes your cubicle and you're shocked back to the harsh reality of that building plan. For a brief moment, though, you acted out a desire by imagining that you were doing so, and in the process gave some fulfillment, if only slight, to that desire.

The process is not radically different for dreams proper. A sleeping child needing to urinate might simply dream about urinating just as she might dream about eating if she experiences a pang of hunger while sleeping. Either of these two dreams might provide partial satisfaction of her bodily needs. Of course, as many children who have wet their beds have learned, if the need to urinate is too great, a dream about doing so will not prevent one's waking up in a soaked bed. For an external stimulus like an alarm clock, Freud will suggest that our minds might interpret the stimulus as church bells and thus as not requiring immediate action (pp. 114–115). Or imagine a sleeping camper whose tent begins to leak during a rainstorm. She might dream she is taking a shower, or playing under a sprinkler, in order to make sense of the sensation of water falling on her skin without having to rouse herself from sleep.

Matters get more interesting when the sleeper is experiencing sexual arousal. Instead of waking up and fulfilling that need with another person or by herself, Freud suggests, the sleeper might achieve partial satisfaction of that need by dreaming that she is having sex. However, Freud observes that many people of his day will be uncomfortable dreaming, for instance, that they are participating in an orgy, or having sex with an individual whom social norms have placed off-limits to them. After all, they might awake to remember this dream and be disturbed to find within themselves such licentious impulses. This is where the process or *distortion* comes into play. One's underlying or, as Freud will say, *latent* desire might be for sexual intercourse; however, our mind, Freud suggests, may distort that desire so that what we experience in the dream is only imperfectly related to that underlying desire. We might as a result dream that we are riding on horseback, or swinging on a swing. These events are a dream's *manifest content*—what we might experience or recall happening as part of the dream's narrative. Freud's intriguing suggestion is that in spite of the distortion that has transformed latent to manifest content, the result might still give the dreamer partial satisfaction of her sexual impulse, and, if all goes well, enough satisfaction that that impulse will not rouse her from sleep. The result will be a compromise: while dreaming sleep is not as restful and rejuvenating as dreamless sleep, it is still better for the organism than waking up.

Related to the two concepts of latent and manifest content are the notions of *dream work* and *dream interpretation*. "Dream work" is Freud's technical term for the process by which the mind transforms latent content to a manifest content that we do not find disturbing. Dream work is not itself a process of which we are aware, but it is a crucial component of the mechanisms that help to protect our sleep from interruption. By contrast, the process of dream interpretation is that means by which a person considers the manifest content of a dream (either her own or someone else's) and discerns the latent content that produced it. Dream interpretation is a bit like detective work, requiring, Freud will tell us, considerable patience and attention to detail.

As we further consider Freud's remarks on dreams, we also discover a theme in his writings according to which dreams have a communicative function for those in whom they occur. I would not be surprised to find that you have had dreams in which something embarrassing happens, and the narrative in which this embarrassment occurs is related to something occurring or about to occur in your waking life. You might be planning to give a speech to your colleagues at work, and dream the night before that speech that while giving it you look down only to find that you've forgotten to put on pants! Or if you're a student preparing for an exam, you dream that you're about to take that exam but cannot find the room in which it is being held or even writing utensils with which to take it. These speech and exam dreams are sometimes called anxiety dreams, and it is not too far-fetched to suppose that they serve to exhort us to prepare for stressful events: be sure to wear pants when you give that speech, and find out where your final exam is taking place and have numerous pens on hand when you go there!

As an example of a dream that sends a message to the dreamer, Freud offers the case of a patient who told him that he dreamt that he was sitting with his family around an irregularly shaped table. The patient then told Dr. Freud that in waking life he had seen just such a peculiarly shaped table at the home of another family, and that he felt that the relationship between the father and son in this family was also peculiar. The patient also told Freud that he felt that he, too, had an odd relationship with his father. Freud remarks, "So the table had been taken into the dream in order to point out this parallel" (ILP, p. 146).

"Pointing out" a parallel or some other state of affairs is a different function from protecting sleep from interruption. Freud also gives no hint that the dreamer was subject to an internal impulse or external event that threatened to interrupt his sleep. Accordingly, Freud's official definition of dreams cited above—the manner in which the mind reacts to stimuli that impinge upon it in the state of sleep by means of hallucinatory satisfaction of our desires—is narrower than his actual theorizing requires. Just as anxiety dreams might help alert us to possible dangers in waking life and make us more vigilantly prepare for them, so too, a dream of the sort just discussed seems primarily aimed at notifying the dreamer of one or more of his unconscious feelings—in this case his feelings about his relationship with his father. This is a communicative function for dreams rather than a function of protecting a valuable process from being interrupted.

It is easy to lose sight of this distinction between two functions of dreams in Freud's treatment because, first of all, he does not revise his definition of dreams to accommodate their communicative function. What is more, he tends to muddy the waters with his talk of "symbolism" in dreams. This talk is both confusing and highly controversial. For instance, in the chapter entitled "Symbolism in Dreams" (Chapter 10 of *ILP*), Freud offers something like a lexicon enabling us to go from a certain item in a dream's manifest content to what he takes it to be a "symbol" of. More often than not, the things symbolized are of a sexual nature. Anything longer than it is wide symbolizes a penis. Any collection of three things (stones, birds, etc.) is a symbol, Freud tells us, of male genitalia, and any item with an identifiable exterior and interior in which something can be placed (like a purse, jewelry box, or even a house) symbolizes the vagina. He continues,

> *Doors* and *gates* . . . are symbols of the [female] genital orifice. Materials, too, are symbols for women: *wood, paper*, and objects made of them, like *tables* and *books*. Among, animals, *snails* and *mussels* at least are undeniably female symbols; among the parts of the body, the *mouth* (as a substitute for the genital orifice); among buildings, *churches* and *chapels*.
> (*ILP*, 192)

The first thing to note is that Freud's use of the word "symbol" here is not limpid. Symbols are crucially bound up with communication: words, phrases, gestures, are central examples, and even when we speak of religious symbolism we tend to have in mind the use of one item (a cross, a scarab beetle, a fish) to represent something else. However, on Freud's approach, if I have a dream in which I am entering a church, that is a manifest content that is the distorted result of a latent desire for sexual intercourse with someone possessing a vagina. The church's appearance in my dream is not designed to convey a message, but rather is the dream's way of preventing my sexual urges from interrupting my sleep; it is no more communicative than a malnourished prisoner's dream in which he eats a sumptuous meal.

Let's continue to use "symbol" as Freud does, but without being misled. The second thing to note is that Freud's claims here are extremely controversial. Suppose I've spent the day exploring tide pools as part of my beach vacation. I've seen starfish, crabs, snails, and mussels. After a fun-filled day I fall asleep and dream about spending more time among the tide pools with these same creatures. Freud will apparently say that the snails and mussels are symbols of female genitalia, and thus that I have a latent desire for sexual contact with female genitalia. This would be so, on his theory, even if I've already had ample sexual contact, and even if another very reasonable explanation of my dream's latent content is presenting itself: namely that I've gained many new experiences over the day and my mind is processing them.

Here I suspect that Freud or one of his followers will suggest that I am exhibiting "resistance." He tends to use this term to refer to any vigorous criticism of his theory: if you challenge it, that must mean you're hiding something—indeed hiding the very thing that the theory is talking about, and so the theory is proven correct after all! In the next section of this chapter we will take a moment to ask whether this strategy is a legitimate way to respond to challenges.

For now, however, let us observe that if Freud is right to think that dreams can have either a sleep-protecting or communicative function, we may still conclude that we can learn about ourselves by remembering our dreams after waking up and scrutinizing them as best we can. For the sleep-protection function of dreams, we use dream interpretation to analyze our way down to their latent content. Once there we might find ourselves concluding that we harbor homosexual desires, or an impulse to destroy someone whom we had been consciously telling ourselves we felt kindly toward. For the "communicative" dreams, we need to decode the message, most likely once again with the aid of dream interpretation. The result here too might contain some hard truths—that our relationship with a parent is abnormal, or that you actually are anxious about something you have to do even though you had not previously admitted it to yourself. In either case you have learned something of value even if the process of achieving that realization might be painful.

Some Epistemological Hijinks

Part of the fascination of Freud's writings is that he is wonderfully artful in making a case for his views. In some respects, that case is clear and potentially quite powerful. For instance, he argues—although he would not put it in these terms—that IBE justifies positing unconscious phenomena since the best explanation of third-personally observable behavior is that it is due to unconscious events or processes. This is an acceptable line of reasoning raising no particular theoretical difficulties. The only question is whether unconscious material, and the particular unconscious material that he posits, really are the best explanation of the phenomena that need to be accounted for.

At the same time, in other passages Freud makes argumentative moves that should raise our concerns. In discussing the "aufstossen" toast, Freud imagines the man who had made it objecting to his analysis of the episode, writing:

> I can imagine the unknown proposer of the toast . . . He gets impatient and suddenly breaks out: "Just you stop trying to cross-question me or I shall turn nasty. You're going to ruin my whole career with your suspicions. I simply said 'aufstossen' instead of 'anstossen' because I'd said 'auf' twice before in the same sentence . . . there's nothing more to be interpreted about it. D'you understand? *Basta!*"
>
> (ILP, 60)

Freud now remarks that this man has a strong interest in our not finding a deeper meaning behind his parapraxis. In a later passage Freud offers the analogy with a child whose fist is tightly clenched: we may feel confident, he suggests, that we will find the child hiding something inside his fingers. More generally, Freud uses the term "resistance" to refer to any energetic denial of his claims about unconscious causes of behavior. (In what follows I will use a capitalized version of this word, "Resistance" to refer to Freud's defined notion. On this usage, all Resistance is resistance, but not vice versa.) As he uses the term and associated concept, Freud seems to hold that whenever there is Resistance, this is merely further confirmation of his theory of the unconscious. Why else, the suggestion seems to be, would the Resistance be so energetic?

Something about this is fishy, however. Suppose I am convinced that aliens have infiltrated our society and are just waiting for the right moment to achieve domination of our entire planet. I also point out that this is a disturbing fact that most people will feel a need to deny, since to accept it portends the destruction of the human race. If you now Resist my claims by energetically pointing out that they are based on no evidence, it surely won't do for me to respond, "Ha, see, your Resistance just goes to prove my point. The end is near!" This is epistemic hijinks that should fool no one. Freud's analogous strategy toward those who challenge his claims about unconscious causes of behavior, is, I submit, equally dubious. This does not mean that those claims are untrue. Rather, it allows us to conclude that this particular strategy for defending them is not persuasive.

We may also see in more detail where Freud's reasoning fails. First of all, one can resist his claims without Resisting his claims. As a neutral, third-party observer to the "Basta!" exchange, we may simply ask Freud, in the calmest way possible, what his evidence is for the interpretation of the young man's slip of the tongue. Surely just asking for evidence for one person's claim about another's behavior does not implicate the questioner as having an ulterior motive? Further, even if we ask for that evidence energetically, and thereby engage in Resistance, it is simply not true that the only possible explanation of that energy is that we are trying to hide something. Another possibility is that we are surprised by, and perhaps even highly skeptical of Freud's claims given other competing explanations of why the man offering the toast said what he did. That again need not implicate us.

Undermining a person's question by contending that the very act of asking it proves your position, is a case of what students of logic and reasoning call an *ad hominem* strategy. Such a strategy characteristically involves criticizing a person's statement, question, challenge or other conversational contribution by criticizing that person herself. Have you ever heard a public figure (or his spokesperson) respond to criticism by claiming that such criticism is "politically motivated"? Suppose the figure in question is the mayor of your town, and that the person he defeated in the last election has criticized his use of public funds for his own personal gain. This sounds like a serious criticism, but the Mayor's office points out that it comes from a source who might have a vested interest in seeing the Mayor fail. Naturally it would be in the interest of the loser to see the incumbent politician taken down from his current position. Such an outcome would be a satisfying vindication for the loser, who might in fact get swept into office on a wave of voter indignation! That may all be true, but it does not show that the critic's accusation may be ignored. Even if the criticism of the mayor's use of public funds flows from less than virtuous motives, it may still be worth investigating. The appropriate response to the critic is not to accuse her of being "politically motivated," but rather to ask her to present her evidence for thinking that public funds have been misappropriated. That evidence should then be assessed on its own merits, and those assessing it may think what they want of the person who made the accusation in the first place.

So too, imagine a person asking Freud to provide evidence for his claim that whenever a group of three items (such as three apples, coins, or airplanes passing overhead) appear in a dream, that group represents male genitalia. This is a fascinating idea, the skeptic might point out, but what reason do we have for thinking it is true? Given his response to similar challenges, we may easily imagine Freud replying that this is a highly *motivated* question, insinuating in the process that the questioner has something to hide, such as a sexual urge that he finds it too painful to acknowledge. We may now see that such a response is little better than the reply that we saw, in the example of the Mayor, that the challenge is politically motivated. After all, someone asking Freud for his evidence in support of his system for interpreting dream symbolism might well be motivated by any number of dubious inclinations. But even if this is so, it would do nothing to undermine the legitimacy of asking for the evidence in support of a claim that is, in the end, empirical.

Let us, then, not be misled by *ad hominem* attacks on those who raise skeptical doubts about Freud's claims. At the same time, we should also note that in certain contexts, a person's credentials do matter for the evaluation of what she says. This is particularly so when we are being asked to accept someone's claim based either on their putative expertise, or on what they allege to have witnessed. A person who claims to be an expert on liver disease tells us that a new drug is highly effective in treating cirrhosis of the liver. But investigative reporting reveals that he is being paid handsomely by the company that developed this drug. That finding should make us look skeptically on his claims, and perhaps seek an independent replication of his results. Again, someone says she saw a man pickpocketing another on a busy sidewalk. This should gain our attention, but if we later learn that the alleged witness has a long of history of fabricating crimes, or has bad eyesight and was not wearing corrective lenses at the time, that too should make us doubtful of the allegation. Notice however that cases such as these involve people asking others to believe their claims (about the efficacy of a drug, or the identity of a pickpocket). By contrast, someone raising a skeptical challenge to Freud is not asking us to take her word for anything, but is rather asking for evidence in support of an intriguing claim. Anyone has a right to ask for such evidence.

I emphasize again that even if Freud's response to some criticisms (both those the he considers in his writing, and those that have in fact been raised by critics) is not cogent, that does not mean that his claims about the unconscious are untrue. For all we have said so far, it may still be true, for instance, that any grouping of three items in a dream represents genitalia. What we need is evidence for believing that such a claim is true.

Searching for Evidence

We have seen how a posit of unconscious phenomena could be made on legitimate evidential grounds: cite the evidence, such as a parapraxis or a dream's manifest content, consider a variety of hypotheses, and show that the simplest hypothesis aiming to explain the phenomenon is one positing unconscious states or events. In principle this is a perfectly legitimate method, though it may be difficult to establish in a given case that a posit of an unconscious cause is really the best explanation compared to others. Freud, however, offers further ways in which he thinks his theory about the unconscious may be supported. One such way is by asking the psychoanalyst's patient whether she agrees with what the theory says about her. Such patients were known as *analysands*, and Freud holds that one way in which we can verify the claims of his theory is to see that on occasion, the analysand does indeed agree that the psychoanalyst's theories about her unconscious mind are correct. "Aha, she might say, you're right that all these years I've been wanting to murder my mother and sleep with my father. That explains everything!" Or, "You've been insisting for some time that my recurring dream about being a concert pianist is a manifestation of an unfulfilled desire to masturbate. Now I see that you've been right all along!"

Such epiphanies as these might look like vindications of Freud's general claims, as well as of particular claims that certain psychoanalysts might make about their patients. However, it is also useful to note that as a practicing therapist himself, Freud was wont to demand quite ferociously to his patients that they were experiencing the unconscious events that he said they were. Such aggressive tactics are more likely to coerce agreement than to help bring the patient to a realization. What is more, even if such aggressive tactics are not used, we do well to ask how many patients do not find themselves agreeing with the therapist's claims about the unconscious causes of their behavior. Not only that, but we should also note that even if the therapist doesn't explicitly suggest an explanation at all, he might still guide the patient's reasoning down a particular path without knowing it. In the famous case of Clever Hans, a horse by that name seemed to be able to do simple addition, such as 3 + 4 or 7 + 2. When asked, "What is 3 + 4?," he would stomp his hoof seven times, and likewise for other simple sums. Amazing! However, it was eventually revealed that what enabled Hans to "count" so well is that he was sensitive to the breathing of his owner, who would take a short breath each time Hans needed to stomp once more to arrive at the desired sum, and then return to breathing as normal. The owner was not aware that he was doing this, but the revelation upended any claims to Hans' mathematical prowess.

So too, a therapist might influence a patient's search for the causes of his behavior without knowing it: breathing, facial expression, tone of voice and a host of other behaviors that he may not produce intentionally, and not even be aware of, might each subtly influence the patient's judgment. Until Freud or those who follow him can provide an experimental setting in which the possibility of such suggestions may be ruled out, a patient's claim to have discovered the true cause of his behavior will be suspect.

Another reason given for the accuracy of psychoanalytic theory comes in the form of an analyst saying that his posits about the unconscious are usually correct, and that he has decades of clinical experience backing up that claim. Let us assume that the clinician who says this is being sincere, and not willfully ignoring many cases in which his posits were incorrect. Even then, such a claim will seem impressive until we consider the various conditions under which it might be made. We are generally prone to remember successes more than failures. Furthermore, according to the phenomenon known as *confirmation bias*, we tend to focus on and remember those cases that confirm our theory and forget those that do not.[4] Drawing general conclusions under such conditions will not be terribly convincing. After all, we can also imagine an astrologer confidently, and even sincerely telling us that she has years of success in predicting people's future based on the position of the stars. So long as we keep in mind how easy it is to forget all the predictions that were not borne out, or that many predictions were so vague that it would have been impossible to falsify them, we should not be impressed by the astrologer's confidence. Why should things be different with psychoanalysts?

Fortunately, in recent years some experimental psychologists have put certain of Freud's theories to empirical test. While I know no study that has attempted to vindicate any particular claims about symbolism in dreams, some psychologists have focused on various of the so-called defense mechanisms that Freud has posited to inquire how well supported these are by modern experimental techniques. One such mechanism is known as *reaction-formation*, that process by which a subject with an unconscious desire strenuously rejects any stimulation that might activate it. Someone with repressed homosexual impulses shows reaction formation, in this sense, if they consciously hold strongly homophobic views. The question is then whether homophobic individuals show evidence of homoerotic tendencies. Adams et al. (1996) set out to determine whether there was an association between homophobic attitudes and homosexual arousal.[5] These researchers recruited male college students, some of whom scored high on a questionnaire measuring homophobia. All such subjects watched sexually explicit videos, some depicting heterosexual acts and others homosexual acts. All the males showed sexual arousal in response to the heterosexual videos. But the homophobic men showed considerably greater sexual arousal to the homosexual videos than did the non-homophobic men. While this study establishes an association between conscious attitudes and sexual impulses, it does not establish a causal connection between the two. However, it is *suggestive* of a causal path since it is difficult to see what else might account for the different patterns of sexual arousal within the group of men studied.

More generally, in an overview of studies attempting to put Freudian theories concerning defense mechanisms to empirical test, the authors Baumeister, Dale, and Sommer (1998) conclude that there is genuine support for the existence of some of these defense mechanisms. They point out, however, that the evidence points to such defense mechanisms being engaged to protect a subject's self-esteem rather than to protect against acknowledgement of disturbing information about sexual or violent impulses.

More broadly, and as we will see in more detail in the next chapter, the last 25 years of research on self-knowledge has tended to support the posit of an unconscious dimension of the human mind. However, this research has abjured a focus on unconscious desires for sexuality and violence, and emphasized instead the importance of efficient negotiation of our physical and perhaps even more importantly, our social environment. In the next chapter we turn to a closer look at this new perspective on the unconscious.

Chapter Summary

- The unconscious is not by definition unknowable. Unconscious material can in principle be known about either by introspective means or by extro-spective means.
- Freud in effect relies on the method of inference to the best explanation as part of his case for what he calls parapraxes.
- This method is particularly powerful when we see a pattern of verbal slips and other behavioral errors, rather than isolated cases.
- Non-conscious phenomena are to be distinguished from unconscious phenomena. The latter are all types of mental states, while the former need not be. Within the realm of the unconscious, we may further distinguish between the pre-conscious and the subconscious.
- In light of his general view of human nature, Freud conjectures that the unconscious mind is the repository of psychological impulses that, if acted on freely, would be corrosive to civilized life. Many norms making up the

fabric of civilized society are precisely designed (if not consciously) to keep these impulses in check.

- Freud offers an account of the function of dreaming as the mind's method of protecting sleep from interruption. This account does not square with all the cases he considers, however, since he also discusses dreams whose function seems to be to send the dreamer a message.
- Freud and those who followed him sometimes indulged in what we have termed epistemic hijinks in responding to those who question their claims. That abuse of the norms of inquiry does not itself show that Freud's claims about the unconscious are untrue.
- Freud's account of dream symbolism is one of the most controversial elements of his position. Nothing in principle prevents investigating some of these claims about dream symbolism experimentally.

Study Questions

1. Could a person know about an unconscious state within her without that state in the process becoming conscious? Please explain you answer.
2. At one point in ILP, Freud remarks that, "we believe that civilization is to a large extent constantly being created anew" (p. 27). What does he mean by this claim, and how does the claim relate to the view he suggests about human nature?
3. Please explain the difference between conscious states and non-conscious states. Are all non-conscious states also unconscious? Please explain your answer. Next, please explain the difference between pre-conscious states and subconscious states, and give an example of each kind.
4. What is the notion of Inference to the Best Explanation, and how is that notion relevant to Freud's attempt to show that parapraxes "have a sense of their own"?
5. Please consider the "Basta!" passage on the bottom of p. 60 of ILP beginning, "H'm! That was a surprising reaction, a truly energetic denial." In this passage Freud uses a rhetorical technique about which we might have doubts. What is this technique, and why we might have doubts about its cogency?
6. What for Freud, is the function of dreams? After distinguishing between his notions of *manifest* and *latent content*, please give an example of a dream and its interpretation that conform to his theory. In your answer be sure to explain the difference between *dreamwork* and *dream interpretation*.
7. What is the example of Clever Hans, and how is it relevant to our discussion of the evidential support for psychoanalysis?
8. What is the notion of Resistance as it has been understood in this chapter? Why might it be thought to be a tool permitting a form of epistemic hijinks?
9. Please explain the Freudian notion of sublimation, and provide an example of that process at work.
10. Consider one of the claims that Freud makes about dream symbolism. Might that claim be experimentally validated? Please explain your answer.

Notes

1. The idea of a Freudian slip is such an accepted part of common sense that an entrepreneur in Eugene, Oregon, has called a lingerie shop by that name, presumably expecting potential customers to get the joke.
2. See for instance J. Sidnell, 'Conversation Analysis,' *Oxford Research Encyclopedia of Linguistics* (http://linguistics.oxfordre.com/view/10.1093/acrefore/9780199384655.001.0001/acrefore-9780199384655-e-40?rskey=IorUad&result=2).
3. It is an empirical question whether watching violent movies or playing violent video games makes people more or less violent in their subsequent behavior. As Bushman et al. (1999), point out, however, the evidence does not support the conclusion that these activities have a cathartic effect.
4. For useful overview of the phenomenon of confirmation bias see M. Oswald and S. Grosjean (2004) "Confirmation Bias," in R. Pohl (ed.) *Cognitive Illusions: A Handbook of Fallacies and Biases in Thinking, Judgment and Memory* (New York: Psychology Press), pp. 79–96.
5. H. Adams, L. Wright, and B. Lohr (1996) "Is Homophobia Associated With Homosexual Arousal?" *Journal of Abnormal Psychology*, vol. 105, pp. 440–5.

Introductory Further Reading

Freeman, L. (1990) *The Story of Anna O.—The Woman Who Led Freud to Psychoanalysis* (St. Paul, MN: Paragon House). Gripping narrative of a case study that was crucial to Freud's development.

Gomez, L. (2005) *The Freud Wars: An Introduction to the Philosophy of Psychoanalysis* (New York and London: Routledge). A discussion of the controversies surrounding the methodologies and empirical foundation of psychoanalysis.

Goode, E. (2001) 'Rats May Dream, It Seems, of Their Days at the Mazes,' *New York Times*. Report on research bearing on the function of dreams to help build memories.

Hobson, J.A. (2011) *Dreaming: A Very Short Introduction* (Oxford: Oxford University Press). Accessible introduction to the nature of dreaming from a neuroscientific point of view.

Lear, J. (2015) *Freud*, 2nd Edition (London and New York: Routledge). Lucid treatment of the life and work of Freud.

Lipton, P. (2000) 'Inference to the Best Explanation,' in W. Newton-Smith (ed.) *A Companion to the Philosophy of Science* (Oxford: Blackwell), pp. 184–93. Accessible explanation of the motivation for and meaning of the principle of inference to the best explanation.

Advanced Further Reading

Baumeister, R., Dale, K., and K. Sommer (1998) 'Freudian Defense Mechanisms and Empirical Findings in Modern Social Psychology: Reaction Formation, Projection, Displacement, Undoing, Isolation, Sublimation, and Denial,' *Journal of Personality*, vol. 66, pp. 1081–124.

Bushman, B., A. Stack, and R. Baumeister. (1999) 'Catharsis, Aggression, and Persuasive Influence: Self-Fulfilling or Self-Defeating Prophecies?' *Journal of Personality and Social Psychology*, vol. 76, pp. 367–76. Experimental investigation of some central Freudian concepts.

Crewes, F. (2006) 'The Unknown Freud,' reprinted in his *The Follies of the Wise: Dissenting Essays* (Emeryville, CA: Shoemaker Hoard), pp. 15–42. Scathing criticism of aspects of Freud's methodology as a clinician.

Dawes, R. (1994) *House of Cards: Psychology and Psychotherapy Built on Myth* (New York: Free Press). Trenchant criticism of the efficacy of psychoanalysis as compared with other forms of talk therapy.

Gardner, S. (1991) 'The Unconscious,' in J. Neu (ed.) *The Cambridge Companion to Freud* (Cambridge: Cambridge University Press). Useful discussion of conceptual issues associated with the unconscious.

Grünbaum, A. (1984) *The Foundations of Psychoanalysis: A Philosophical Critique* (Berkeley: University of California Press). Monumental and wide-ranging attack on psychoanalysis' methodology.

Hobson, J.A. (1989) *The Dreaming Brain: How the Brain Creates Both the Sense and Nonsense of Dreams* (New York: Basic Books). An approach to the nature and function of dreams written by a neuroscientist.

Macmillan, M. (1991) *Freud Evaluated: The Completed Arc* (North-Holland: Kluwer). Trenchant criticism of core tenets of psychoanalysis.

Rock, A. (2004) *The Mind at Night: The New Science of How and Why We Dream* (New York: Basic Books). Detailed but accessible review of recent research on the nature and function of dreams.

Weston, D. (1998) 'The Scientific Legacy of Sigmund Freud: Toward a Psychodynamically Informed Psychological Science,' *Psychological Bulletin*, vol. 124, pp. 333–71. Sustained attempt to evaluate the empirical basis for many of the core posits of psychoanalytic theory.

Internet Resources

Thornton, S. (n.d.) 'Sigmund Freud,' in *The Internet Encyclopedia of Philosophy* (www.iep.utm.edu/freud/). Useful general introduction to Freud's thought.

5   The Adaptive Unconscious

Introduction

In this chapter we introduce the last two decades of research offering empirical support for mechanisms governing action, facial recognition, language processing, and many other aspects of competence in both the physical and social worlds. Researchers have provided striking insights into our tendencies to be influenced by factors outside our conscious awareness, or at least outside the focus of our attention—and they do so with the validated methods of experimental psychology and cognitive neuroscience. We will consider evidence for a "psychological immune system" that enables us to put a positive spin on information about ourselves, as well as for the phenomenon of implicit bias that has come to carry new urgency amid heightened attention to racism and other forms of bigotry worldwide. In addition, we will consider recent investigations in the neuroscience of agency to determine whether they pose a challenge to our traditional notion(s) of freedom of will. One common theme emerging from these recent developments is that introspection is at best a weak source of knowledge of oneself. This, however, leaves open the possibility of knowing oneself by "looking outward," and we accordingly explore that route to self-knowledge.

Automaticity and the Adaptive Unconscious

We process a great deal of information without paying much attention to the fact that we are doing so. One glance at your friend's face will usually be enough to tell if she is amused or irritated by the image she just saw on her phone. Likewise, as you gaze out the window from the bus you are riding in, so long as the words on the billboard are not unfamiliar, and the grammar of the phrase or sentence is not confusing, you effortlessly understand the message aimed at you. In fact, for those billboards or signs that are in a language we speak fluently, if we so much as look at them, we cannot choose *not* to understand their message, and this is so even if we find the message annoying or even offensive. All this occurs in spite of the fact that even though we are familiar with the words and grammar of what is on the sign, we most probably have never seen that particular message before. As a result, it is not likely that we understand the sign simply by association with previous experience. Instead, and in light of the best evidence available from modern linguistics, most of us engage on a daily basis in a complex process of language comprehension by virtue of which we detect a noun phrase ("Bob's burgers," for instance), then a verb phrase ("are the best in Uruguay"), and then link them together to produce a complex meaning ("Bob's burgers are the best in Uruguay"). No doubt, most of us do this without knowing the terms "noun phrase" and "verb phrase."

The above comprehension process all happens virtually instantaneously and without our being aware of exerting any effort. Compare that with trying to interpret a sentence in a language you are just starting to learn: you struggle to identify one part of speech, and then another, and then have to think about how they link up to produce a complex meaning. By now you may have forgotten the meaning of the first part of speech you identified, and might even abort the process with a headache and the need to take a walk. When language comprehension is not working well, as in this case, we can appreciate how complex the process is when things are going smoothly.

These phenomena suggest that unconscious and automatic processes operate in ways broader than the scope granted them in psychoanalytic theory. Recent experimental psychology has indeed carried on where psychoanalytic theory left off in providing a new approach to the unconscious. Whereas the psychoanalytic movement posited unconscious phenomena that were centered around human impulses toward sexuality and violence, new research emphasizes the power of the unconscious to help us negotiate the world, both natural and social, in ways that would be overwhelmingly cumbersome if we were to do it all consciously. Further, this new research program does its best to ground its claims about the unconscious in rigorous experiments. In response to challenges to support her claims about the unconscious, the defender of what is sometimes called the *adaptive unconscious* will show you the results of her experiments or direct you to those of others.[1] What she will not do is accuse you of Resistance or engage in some other form of epistemic hijinks. In this chapter we will consider some evidence for the existence of the adaptive unconscious, and on that basis reflect on the view of ourselves that this phenomenon suggests.

Researchers hypothesize that by outsourcing much of our cognitive and other mental processing to parts of the mind not needing conscious attention, we become more efficient in negotiating the physical and social words. This outsourcing process is thought to have occurred both in our evolutionary past (phylogeny), as well as in an individual's development (ontogeny), although in different ways in these two cases. For the phylogenetic story, this efficiency provided our hominid ancestors a survival advantage by enabling them to conduct much reasoning—such as determining the distance of objects in the perceptual environment, or sizing up the face of another human being to discern whether they are dangerous or helpful—automatically and effortlessly, freeing up conscious attention for more complex and novel problems. For the ontogenetic story, the adaptive unconscious plays a crucial role in guiding us through everyday activities that were once acquired through careful practice and repetition: reading, riding a bicycle, playing a piano sonata are all painstakingly acquired skills, but once acquired and kept fresh with occasional practice they can generally be carried out with little conscious effort.

Researchers interested in the adaptive unconscious also think of it as *automatic*. This word is used to capture the idea that these unconscious processes proceed without our making any effort. For most of us, multiplying a pair of two digit numbers in our head takes effort and attention, so too with memorizing a phone number or a new acquaintance's name. By contrast, automatic processes do not require exertion on our part, but instead play out unless we make a special effort to stop them. In some cases I may be able to overpower an automatic, unconscious process by distracting myself with something even more intense such as loud music or an electric shock. It would be a mistake, that is, to assume that because they are automatic, unconscious processes are beyond one's control and thus responsibility. We will return to this point when we consider the phenomenon of implicit attitudes.

Once acquired, automatic, unconscious processes can be hard to change. As we settle into adulthood we tend to acquire emotional habits that guide our interpretation of social situations. Often those situations are ambiguous in that it is possible to interpret them in more than one way, where one interpretation might reflect positively while another would reflect poorly on us. Consider the following scenario:

Cubicle Compliment

Your boss Lakshmi comes by and praises your colleague George sitting at the next cubicle for an excellent quarterly report, but she says nothing to you. Here are some things that might run through your head as the boss walks away:

a. I'm proud of George for such excellent work. Props to him!
b. Lakshmi is definitely playing favorites. My report was just as good as George's.
c. I need to keep on doing my best. With any luck my work will be appreciated soon, too.

Your interpretation of this ambiguous social interaction might happen so quickly that you have trouble noticing yourself constructing it. However, how you interpret it might say a good deal about how you tend to respond to others. Many adults interpret ambiguous social cues in characteristic and chronic ways: some tend to see themselves as insufficiently appreciated, while others suffer from an "imposter's syndrome" in which they feel inadequate to the task before them and are forever expecting to be unmasked as incompetent; yet others seem always to take credit for things that go well but never accept any blame when things go poorly. By the time we settle into adulthood, many of us will have acquired habits of the heart that lead us to interpret ambiguous situations in fairly predictable ways. Those ways are on the whole automatic and occur outside the focus of conscious awareness.

As another example of automatic processing, observe that sometimes understanding an utterance also requires recognizing the intentions behind it. Suppose you send a friend a message asking him to join you for a movie in town this evening. Your friend replies: "I've got a big test in my physics class tomorrow." You will probably interpret your friend as meaning without saying that he can't join you for the movie. But how? After all, that message was not part of the conventional meaning of what he said in reply to your invitation. All your friend literally said was that he's got a test tomorrow. Well, presumably after reading his reply you reasoned that he wants to study hard for his physics test, and that tonight will be his last good opportunity to do so. But, you might also have reasoned, one cannot study for a physics test and go to a movie in the same evening: either activity will take many hours of "mono-tasking". As a result, your friend must have meant, in saying what he did, that he will be unable to join you for the movie. But this entire reasoning process likely took place in the blink of an eye, and did not require intellectual exertion on your part in anything like the way that mental math or remembering an old schoolmate's name might. What is more, it would make no difference to the ease of this process if it were carried out unconsciously (either at the pre- or sub-conscious level) or instead in the background of conscious awareness. What matters for its efficiency is its automaticity, not its being unconscious (if it is).

Before examining the empirical evidence in favor of the adaptive unconscious, however, we need to be on our guard against overblown claims about its extent as compared with that of the conscious mind. Timothy Wilson, in his book, *Strangers to Ourselves: Exploring the Adaptive Unconscious* (2002), reminds us that some in the psychoanalytic tradition use an iceberg metaphor for the relation of the conscious to the unconscious parts of the mind: the iceberg's tip is to consciousness as the iceberg's submerged part is to the unconscious. Wilson contends that if we appreciate the extent of the adaptive unconscious, we will conclude that this analogy actually understates matters, and that a better metaphor will be that of a snowball on the tip of that iceberg! This is quite a dramatic claim, suggesting as it does that conscious awareness is only a tiny fraction of mentality. What could justify such a claim? One argument that Wilson offers in its favor is the following:

> Consider that at any given moment, our five senses are taking in more than 11,000,000 pieces of information. Scientists have determined this number by counting the receptor cells each organ has and the nerves that go from these cells to the brain. Our eyes alone send over 10,000,000 signals to our brain each second. Scientists have also tried to determine how many of these signals can be processed consciously at any given time, by looking

at such things as how quickly people can read, consciously detect different flashes of light, and tell apart different kinds of smells. The most liberal estimate is that people can process consciously about 40 pieces of information each second. Think about it: we take in 11,000,000 pieces of information each second, but can process only 40 of them consciously. What happens to the other 10,999,960? It would be terribly wasteful to design a system with such incredible sensory acuity but very little capacity to use the incoming information. Fortunately, we do make use of a great deal of this information outside of conscious awareness.

(Wilson 2004, p. 24)

Although he does not say so explicitly, Wilson strongly suggests that the 10,999,960 bits of information he mentions are processed not only out of conscious awareness, but also unconsciously. This conclusion does not follow from the evidence he provides. The reason is that before drawing the conclusion that he appears to, Wilson would also need to rule out another possibility, namely that the remaining 10,999,960 are processed *non*-consciously. Recalling from our last chapter, "conscious" and "unconscious" do not constitute an exhaustive dichotomy. To be either conscious or unconscious, a thing must still be a mental process or event. Given what we also discussed in Chapter 2, this means that to be mental, an event or process must be cognitive, affective, or experiential. Accordingly, Wilson would need to show that each of the 10,999,960 events he mentions is either cognitive, affective, or experiential. There is, however, little reason to think that, for instance, the stimulation of a receptor cell in one's retina is any of these. That is not to say that the stimulation of a rod or cone in one's retina does not in any way contribute to mental phenomena. Although it is not known precisely how this works, presumably thousands, or hundreds of thousands, of such stimulations, together with the complex series of processes going from the visual cortex to other parts of the brain, together produce a visual experience. But even if a single visual experience is in some sense constituted by hundreds of thousands of individual events at the cellular level, it does not follow that each of these individual events is also a visual experience. (Application of a property to a complex object does not guarantee that it will apply to any of its components: the heap of sand is large, but that does not imply that any of the grains of sand that make it up is large.) So too, contributing to a mental phenomenon does not make an event itself a mental phenomenon. The delivery by red blood cells of oxygen to a neuron in the cerebral cortex very likely contributes to mentality in some way: perhaps there is a thought, emotion, mood, or experience that it facilitates. But that does not mean that the oxygen delivery is itself a mental event, any more than the production of new skin cells as my body repairs a wound, is a mental event.

The foregoing argument for the vastness of the unconscious mind is not successful. Further, according to the "adaptive unconscious" approach, what enables mental processes to be carried out so efficiently as to give us a survival advantage is not their being unconscious; rather, it is their being automatic. For all proponents of the adaptive unconscious approach have said, there may be processes that are in the background of conscious awareness but that are not the focus of our attention. So long as they proceed automatically, they will still be carried out with speed and efficiency. Just as your overall experience at a given time might contain sensations to which you are not attending (the sound of the fan blowing in the next room, or the experience of the chair on which you're sitting exerting pressure on your legs), you may engage in reasoning processes without paying attention to the fact that you are doing so. Provided that such processes are automatic, they will be carried out efficiently.

Learning, Emoting, Goal-Setting, and "Somatic Markers"

Let us not be quick to overestimate either the magnitude or even the unconsciousness of the adaptive unconscious. Instead let us consider further evidence in favor of the phenomenon. Here are three types:

Unconscious learning: Edouard Claparède (1911/1951) was a French physician, one of whose patients was amnesiac. In particular, this patient could not form new memories even if she retained some memories from her distant past. Consequently, whenever Claparède visited this patient, she would not recall having seen him before and he would have to re-introduce himself. On one occasion, Claparède greeted his patient with a hand that concealed a small pin; the patient started back in pain and confusion. On subsequent occasions, she had no memory of having met the doctor before, but she refused to shake his hand. This suggests that the patient had learned from experience that shaking hands with this doctor was dangerous even though she was not conscious of having learned this. Further, and bearing in mind the danger of confusing non-conscious with unconscious events, it is also plausible that the patient had undergone an unconscious rather than a non-conscious process: after all, learning results in new knowledge, and knowledge—or at least propositional knowledge—presupposes the cognitive state of belief.

More recent research has continued to support the existence of unconscious learning. Reber (1989) reports studies in which subjects were presented with strings of letters that were constructed (unbeknownst to the subjects) according to precise rules. Subjects were then asked to memorize about 20 of these strings. After that, subjects were presented with strings of letters in combinations they had not seen before and asked which of them conformed to the rules used to generate the strings they had memorized earlier. Subjects did significantly better than chance at telling which strings did in fact conform to the artificial grammar. Yet subjects had little success when asked to verbally formulate the rules that generated the strings they thought were acceptable. As Reber (1989) reports, the result has been replicated by numerous other researchers. The implication seems to be that we can learn rules without being aware that we are doing so.

Unconscious emoting: Researchers can activate a person's emotions in experimental settings by flashing words before her eyes but at such a short duration that they cannot perceive those words consciously. Zemack-Rugar and colleagues (2007) did just this with words associated with the emotions of guilt and sadness. For guilt, they flashed the words "guilty," "blameworthy," "guilt-ridden," and "culpable," and then showed subjects the nonsense string "XQFBZRMQWGBX," which served as a mask. This string was also used to mask words used to activate sadness, namely "sad," "miserable," "depressed," and "gloomy." Participants were then asked to allocate a specified amount of money between two options: CDs and DVDs, on the one hand, and school supplies on the other. At least for those subjects who scored high on an independent measure of the extent to which they were prone to guilt, when primed with guilt-inducing words, they were more likely to buy school supplies than CDs or DVDs, which they took to be indulgences. More precisely, they were more likely to buy school supplies than they were when primed instead with sadness-inducing words or neutral words such as "balanced," "neutral," "regular," "ordinary." Analogous results were produced when subjects were primed in similar ways but given the opportunity to help others in need: those who were guilt-prone were more likely to help others when subliminally primed with guilt-associated words. The implication that Zemack-Ruger and colleagues draw is that we can be influenced emotionally without being consciously aware of this fact, but in ways that nevertheless affect our behavior.

Unconscious goal-setting: Bargh et al. (2001) report experiments where subjects were asked to complete a word-search puzzle in which certain of the terms they needed to find concerned high performance (such as "strive," "attain," "achieve"), while others were asked to search for more neutral words such as "ranch," "carpet," "river," and "shampoo." Those primed with the first set of words were more likely to complete other word-search puzzles more successfully, were more likely to keep working on such puzzles even when they were told by experimenters to stop, and to resume work on the puzzle after an interruption. Yet they had no conscious awareness of being influenced by these priming words. Similarly, in a related set of experiments, subjects were primed with words having to do with cooperation ("cooperative," "fair," "friendly," "share") as opposed to more neutral words ("umbrella," "city," "gasoline," "wet"). Those who had been primed with the cooperative words were in fact more likely to cooperate with others on a resource-allocation task, even though once again they had no conscious awareness of having been influenced by the priming words.

As these examples suggest, an array of fairly sophisticated mental processes can occur outside of our conscious awareness. But unlike unconscious impulses toward sexuality and violence, such unconscious phenomena are not inherently a challenge to civilized society as the psychoanalytic movement proposed. Nor is it the case that we would be better off if we could bring such processes into conscious awareness, any more than it would be for a doctor's office to do all of its billing in-house rather than outsource it to a firm that specializes in billing medical patients. Rather, so long as the service is providing a cost-effective alternative to the physician, she is likely better off outsourcing the work and then forgetting about it as much as possible. So too, we benefit from the automation of mental processing so long as doing so enables our conscious minds to concentrate on problems that are novel and challenging.

One mechanism that may enable many of the above effects is known as the *somatic marker*. *Soma* is a Greek word for body, and the term "somatic marker" suggests a process by which our bodies mark items of experience. The idea of a somatic marker is similar to that of a gut feeling, in that both are manifestations of our body's reactions to external stimuli. However, somatic markers are understood in terms of how we react to items of experience, be it through perception, imagination, or memory. (This feature, by contrast, is not obviously built into that of a gut feeling.) As we will see, somatic markers may also be highly adaptive (at both the phylogenetic and ontogenetic levels), in that they facilitate split-second decision-making rather than requiring painstaking, cost-benefit calculation. It is less clear, however, that somatic markers must be unconscious.

If you are afraid of spiders, then even a small and relatively harmless spider will stand out for you perceptually: you can only look at it *fearfully*, so that it appears to loom, seeming as if it is about to deliver a vicious attack. You may not even be able to think about a hypothetical spider without a spike in blood pressure, increase in skin conductivity, or some other physiological indication of fear. So too, someone who is clinically depressed might experience everything around him as dark and bereft of life. The prospect of tasks such as cleaning his house or making dinner might seem so daunting that neither gets done, and instead filth accumulates and he lives on junk food. Similar phenomena arise for those who are neither phobic nor depressed: imagine an old romantic interest of yours walks into a room where you are. Even if you are only aware of that person through peripheral vision, their image might still pulse with intensity compared with everyone else. Or you open your e-mail to see that your inbox contains a message from a company you've applied to for a job: will this be an invitation to an interview, or a rejection? Until you click on the message, you may not know the answer, but the subject-line of that e-mail will stand out for you as vividly as a spider does for a person who is arachnophobic.

The hypothesis that much of our experience is marked somatically is due to Damasio (1994), who argues that this fact is crucial to our being able to negotiate our way effectively through the world. His reason is that so long as you have somatically marked the world properly, such markers can serve as guides to action. Someone properly brought up will refrain from stealing, at least in part because they somatically mark the image of their own hypothetical mugshot in local the newspaper with horror or revulsion. Someone raised in a culture that is not dysfunctional, and who is herself neurotypical, will look upon the prospect of child sexual abuse with (at the very least) disgust. Likewise, Damasio offers the following scenario:

> Imagine yourself as the owner of a large business, faced with the prospect of meeting or not with a possible client who can bring large business but who also happens to be the archenemy of your best friend, and proceeding

or not with a particular deal. The brain of a normal, intelligent, and educated adult reacts to the situation by rapidly creating scenarios of possible
response options *and* outcomes.

(1994, p. 170)

Damasio does not offer his opinion about the right thing to do in this situation.
He does, however, urge that an effective way of deciding what would be the
right choice for you is to consult how your mind somatically marks the potential
outcomes of the various choices you might make. Visualize yourself shaking
hands in the dappled sunlight of an outdoor café as you close a deal with this
new client: now your best friend walks by and sees the handshake. How is that
prospect somatically marked for you? If it is marked in a strongly negative
way, then that is good reason to think that you should avoid making the deal.

More generally, if Damasio's somatic marker hypothesis is correct, then our
perceptual world (including what we experience in memory and contemplation of the future) is made not just of colors, sounds, shapes, and textures (the
primary and secondary qualities of Descartes), but also items of bodily significance: you see that the thing over there is a book, but you cannot but do so
without a twinge of guilt, since you've borrowed it from a friend and she needs
it back; and you hear that buzzing on your phone, but do so with a gush of pleasure since you expect it to be a message from someone you love and expect to
see soon. Further, so long as we are neurally healthy and raised in societies that
are not dysfunctional in some way, those bodily reactions to items of experience
are reliable signposts telling us what to do.[2]

Opinions and theories will differ as to whether somatic markers are conscious
or not. It does seem clear that one can experience an object as somatically
marked without noticing that one is doing so: I hear the knock on the door *with
trepidation*, but perhaps do not notice that this is how I am experiencing the
event. Instead, my mind might be preoccupied with panic-stricken calculation
of how I should hide from these unwanted visitors. According to the Higher-
Order Thought (HOT) theory of consciousness, for a mental event M to be
conscious is precisely for it to be the subject matter of a higher-order thought,
M1, which in effect reports, "I am in mental state M." Likewise, for M1 to be
conscious is for it to be the subject of a yet higher, higher-order thought, M2,
which is directed upon M1, and so on. The only upper limit on the level of
thoughts that can be conscious is our cognitive processing capacities. According to the HOT theory of consciousness, then, an item of experience may be
somatically marked without being conscious, since it might not be the subject
of a higher-order thought. Other theories of consciousness that focus more
on whether one is undergoing an experience regardless of whether it is being
attended to by a higher-order thought, will treat somatic markers as conscious.
Rather than try to settle debates about the nature of consciousness, let us simply
note that somatic markers may be consciously experienced. At the very least
they are not inherently subconscious, and only on some theories will they in
some cases be pre-conscious.[3]

A Different Kind of Immune System

Outsourcing the work of conscious attention is not the only role for the adaptive unconscious. Wilson (2002) argues that it also provides us with what he terms a *psychological immune system*. We know that the human body contains powerful resources for protecting us from pathogens: soon after something unusual is detected, our bloodstream quickly delivers antibodies that surround and attack it to the best of their ability. A great deal of our physical health depends on a robust physiological immune system. Wilson's novel suggestion is that one job of the adaptive unconscious is to protect us from threats to our *psychological* equilibrium. You may have suffered one or two setbacks in your life: perhaps a person you asked out on a date did not return the romantic interest, you applied for a job that you did not get, or tried to paint a picture that inspired a passerby to suggest you keep your daytime job! In fact, if you're at all typical, threats to your self-esteem are common. But you may also have noticed that many of us are adept at responding to those threats in ways that protect our self-esteem. In response to the romantic rejection you might think to yourself, "Maybe he's not my type anyway," and rather than responding to the failed job application by concluding that you're destined for un- or marginal employment, you might observe that there are a lot of talented people out there and you might just not have been the best fit for that particular employer. And maybe you will agree with the passerby that the beret and watercolors are best kept for the weekends.

"Spinning" your failures into successes, or at least into non-failures, makes a certain amount of sense. Even when the truth about ourselves is not quite so rosy, seeing ourselves as attractive, professionally successful, and talented most likely encourages us to reach higher and do more than we otherwise might. Like a placebo without the pill, it also gives us the confidence to try again when new romantic, employment, or artistic opportunities present themselves. Our tendency to spin can also, however, be taken too far. You may have known people whose lives have stalled, and who are forever explaining away their failures as due to everyone in the world but them: the subway always makes them late for interviews, no one appreciates their true talents which after all are way ahead of their time, and maybe they are just too refined for this coarse and vulgar world! Such people seem to have over-active psychological immune systems, which helps blind them to some hard truths about their own shortcomings.

In one of the most eloquent passages of *Strangers to Ourselves*, Wilson refers to tension between the psychological immune system and the need for accuracy as "one of the major battlegrounds of the self" (p. 39). On the one hand, a frank acknowledgment of one's own foibles and limitations will likely help one negotiate potentially challenging situations. Knowing that I tend to get nervous in a crowd, I might take this into account and plan accordingly: avoid crowds, or at least make sure I've got some way of escaping it if I know I must be in one, and so forth. On the other hand, "spinning" situations in our favor, at least within limits, seems to have value. In response to the Cubicle Compliment scenario describe above, I hope you'll agree that response C ("I need to keep on doing my best. With luck my work will be appreciated soon, too"), is reasonably constructive, while response A ("I'm proud of George for such excellent work. Props to him!") is probably the most generous. At the same time, spinning too dramatically threatens to make us break free from reality. A fourth response to the ambiguous situation presented in Cubicle Compliment might have been:

> d. Obviously Lakshmi thinks my work is so outstanding that she doesn't want to mention it now since it will make others feel bad!

Unless one has strong evidence that (d) is the right interpretation of the situation, adopting it will threaten to put one out of touch with the situation at work.

It does indeed seem that no small part of coming to know ourselves consists in striking this balance between putting a positive spin on things, and being realistic. Another challenge to being realistic involves our ability to predict how well we will adjust to possible future events. The topic of *affective forecasting* concerns our ability accurately to predict how such future events will affect us. It is all too tempting to think that if only we could: win the lottery, buy that new car, get an invitation to that exclusive night club . . . we would finally be happy. On the other side, we tend to overestimate the extent to which negative events will bring us down. The reason for the latter kind of overestimation, to use terminology from Wilson and Gilbert (2005), is *immune neglect*: we are not cognizant of the robustness of our psychological immune system as a defense against negative events.

We have already mentioned habits of the heart. This is just one way of expressing the idea that personality traits tend to be relatively stable over time for most of us, even though we are not aware of this fact. The chronic nature of personality traits explains why, if you are a generally morose person, winning a large lottery will fill you with euphoria for a short period of time, but that feeling won't last: in not too long your new yacht won't feel fast or sleek enough, and all your new acquaintances will seem like sunshine friends. At the same time, if you're already a sunny person, a windfall will also provide you with some short-term delight, but in the fullness of time won't leave you noticeably sunnier than you were before.

This bit of self-blindness to which most of us are prone has everyday implications. Advertisers often sell not just products, but lifestyles. A car commercial tries to convince you that you can and should achieve the lifestyle of the people depicted in it: rugged outdoor type, sleek urban sophisticate, as the case may be. The implication is that if you buy this car, you will also buy this lifestyle. But if you are in the habit of spending your spare time on the couch watching televised sports, buying a rugged pickup truck is not likely to change you into someone who spends weekends fly-fishing in a trackless wilderness. So too, and more dramatically, people who have to make major health decisions may shrink from choices that could extend their lives due to not appreciating their ability to adapt to, say, being bound to a wheelchair. As Halpern and Arnold (2008) note, not just patients, but also their health care providers, do well to take note of the fact that people are not particularly good at predicting how they will adjust to changes such as losing a limb. (In fact most of us would adjust quite well. Forget the limb if keeping it puts your life at risk!)

The "Illusion of Conscious Will"

A deep feature of our conception of ourselves is that we take our conscious decisions to have important consequences for what we do. Under normal circumstances, it would seem undeniable that my conscious decision made while getting dressed in the morning is what determines whether I put on orange socks or blue socks; later, my conscious decision will settle the matter of whether I have a sandwich or a salad for lunch. Likewise for the more momentous choices: unless I am acting under duress (such as might be produced by severe financial pressure), it would seem indisputable that whether I choose to pursue a career in law, or instead in health care, is determined at least in part by what I decide. However, some authors impressed with both the sophistication of the adaptive unconscious and the range of activities to which it applies, have challenged the idea that our conscious minds have any causal role to play in our behavior. This challenge might be developed on general grounds, or in light of specific experimental results. The general challenge might be put as follows. A scientifically rigorous view of our behavior requires seeing it as caused by nothing other than states of our central nervous system. Thus no divine intervention or anything else supernatural can have a role to play in bringing about what we do. However, if that is right, then our behavior flows entirely from internal, physical causes. And if *that* is so, then it seems to follow that there is no room for conscious decision-making to play a role in bringing about what we do. The psychologists Daniel Wegner and Thalia Wheatley formulate similar reasoning:

> The very notion of the will seems to contradict the core assumption of psychological science. After all, psychology examines how behavior is caused by mechanisms—the rattling off of genetic, unconscious, neural, cognitive, emotional, social, and yet other chains that lead, dully or not, to the things people do. If the things we do are caused by such mechanisms, how is it that we sometimes experience willfully doing them?
>
> (Wegner and Wheatley (1999)

These authors are assuming in this passage that if agents did have a will that was at least occasionally responsible for our actions, that will would have either to be non-physical in the sense of that notion proposed by Descartes; or, if it is was physical, it would have to stand partly outside the causal order: it might cause bodily movements, but it will not be caused by anything within our bodies. From this assumption, together with the other considerations they cite, Wegner and Wheatley infer that our experience of consciously willing actions must be illusory: consciously willing an action is always causally inert. The only question that remains is under what conditions do we *experience* ourselves as consciously willing our actions. In so doing, however, these authors are presupposing a controversial philosophical assumption.

The assumption in question is that an event of consciously willing an action cannot be both a physical and a mental event, and at the same time have physical causes. This assumption is dubious. To see why, consider lightning, which is the transmission of electrons between the earth's surface and its atmosphere. A single stroke of lightning might also be an event that is beautiful and scary. One and the same event, then, might be truly described as both the transmission of electrons, and as being scary. The lightning will still be a physical process with physical causes and effects; it simply has other properties as well, such as aesthetic ones. So too, a particular activation of neurons is a physical event with a physical cause. However, it might also have mental properties, such as being a decision to bite into an apple or to wiggle one's finger. This is not to say that all neural processes are also mental events: avoiding this conclusion is one of the lessons we gained from our discussion of the long passage from Wilson, concerning the snowball-on-top-of-the-iceberg metaphor, quoted above. Yet if we are inclined toward a materialist monist view of the mind, it will be natural to express this view as the idea that some events are both patterns of neural stimulation and mental events.

You might reply that even if an event of consciously willing an action is both physical and mental, if it does have a physical cause it is not at all clear how it can be free. Doesn't an event's being caused prevent it from being free? Two replies are pertinent here. First of all, the issue of freedom of will need not arise if we are concerned only with the question whether conscious decisions or volitions can bring about effects on our behavior. Our question was about the efficacy of our decisions, not whether we possess freedom of will. And it is not at all clear why an event's being both a neural event and a conscious experience would prevent it from having causal powers.

Second, if we do choose to raise the question of freedom of will that has been lurking in the background, we need to approach it with care, including some terminology for clarification. Let us start with the thesis of *Universal Determinism* (UD), according to which every physical event in the history of the world has a prior, sufficient, physical condition. UD by itself, if true, would not imply that there are no free actions. That conclusion would only follow if we add a further premise known as *Incompatibilism*: there can be no free actions in a world in which UD is true, or, equivalently, UD and freedom of action are incompatible with one another. Notice that an Incompatibilist might turn things around and urge that since (as might seem self-evident to her upon introspection) there are free actions, UD must be false. (Such a view is known as Libertarianism—a term not to be confused with the political movement of the same name.)

But why should we accept Incompatibilism in the first place? According to our everyday use of the notion of acting freely, an action of mine is not free if it is coerced, either by an external force (such as when someone else overpowers me and causes me to pull a gun's trigger) or an internal force, such as when an unexpected and overpowering muscle spasm makes my fist strike your arm. These are extreme cases of coercion, one with an external, the other with an internal source. We are familiar with less extreme cases as well, such as when someone threatens me with bodily harm unless I hand over my wallet. The first two cases are clear instances in which my action is not free, while reasonable people can disagree over whether my handing over my wallet to the assailant is a free action. However, nothing in our common sense notion of a free action would suggest that such an action is coerced simply because it had a prior, sufficient, physical condition. Sheer causation is not, on its own, tantamount to coercion.

In challenging the Incompatibilist assumption that Wegner and Wheatley are unwittingly making in the argument quoted above, I am offering an alternative known as *Compatibilism*: free acts can occur in a world in which UD is true. This alternative is, I contend, supported by common sense. That does not mean that it cannot be challenged. But it does mean that if you're going to argue that a scientific picture of human agency precludes the existence of free actions, you will have to do more than simply assume Incompatibilism: you'll need to argue for it.

So much for the general challenge to the causal efficacy of conscious will. What about more specific challenges? One such challenge points to experimental results suggesting that in some cases, our conscious decisions (or at least our experience of making such decisions) are less efficacious than we might take them to be. In one famous series of studies, Benjamin Libet and colleagues set up experimental subjects in such a way that it was possible to track patterns of activity in their brains.[4] At the same time Libet asked subjects to look at a very large and accurate clock. Then he instructed them to wiggle a finger whenever they felt ready to do so, but to pay close attention to the time (as indicated by the clock) at which they decided to do so, and to make a mental note of that time.

The results were striking. Libet knew about an independently established phenomenon known as the Readiness Potential, or RP, a pattern of neural activity that spikes about 550 ms (milliseconds) before muscles are activated to produce a bodily movement such as a wiggling finger. Further, the subjects in this experiment reported times at which they decided to wiggle their fingers, and on this basis Libet was able to discern that the decision to do so was made approximately 350 ms after the RP and 200 ms before the muscle activation. It thus appears that the RP spikes before the decision to perform the action! One is tempted to suppose that *first* the brain decides to act, and *then* slightly later we experience the sense of making a decision. But if that is right, our experience of consciously deciding what to do seems to occur after the train of agency has left the station. If that train were an old-fashioned steam engine, then the conscious decision might look like the steam coming out of its smokestack: that decision results from neural processes but does not itself cause any of those processes.

It has become popular in recent years to point to studies like those of Libet and pronounce that freedom of will is a quaint, outdated illusion that it is high time to give up. Better to face the hard truth we are no more free than are plants or clouds! One can even find recent books with titles such as "My Brain Made Me Do It!"[5]—the implication being that if my brain made me do it, then I did not. However, as we have already seen, the fact that my action had a neural cause does not itself show that it could not also have had a mental cause: we've just proposed that some events could be both neural and mental. The question is not whether my action had its source in my brain, but whether it had a source in my brain in such a way as to render my consciously willing that action somehow causally inert. Does the priority of the RP to the self-reported time of decision do this? Neuroscience has established that the spiking of an RP predicts that the organism is going to do *something*: it's ready for action, though it has not yet been specified what. One cannot predict from the spiking of an RP just what the organism will do. Perhaps an occurrence of the event of consciously willing is what is required to determine what will be done? To stick with our locomotive metaphor, the suggestion would be that while the RP's spiking shows that the train has left the station, it is approaching a fork in the track at which it could be shunted in any of numerous directions. The organism may now need an event of consciously willing one action or another to determine which track the train will go down. In an extreme case, the organism may need to call upon conscious will to veto action altogether.

What we have observed so far suggests that certain arguments for the inertness of conscious will are not successful. It does not follow that we are always correct when we are take our acts of consciously willing an action to be efficacious. Indeed, some ingenious experiments have shown that we are susceptible to error in such matters. Brasil-Neto et al. (1992), for instance, magnetically stimulated the motor strip in the brains of experimental subjects in either one hemisphere or the other.[6] These researchers also asked subjects to move either their right or left index finger. The externally produced stimulation resulted in a strong tendency in subjects to move their finger contralateral to (on the opposite side of their body from) the hemisphere stimulated. For instance if the left hemisphere was magnetically stimulated, subjects would feel a strong urge to move the finger on the right hand. Nevertheless, whether they received this stimulation or not, subjects reported feeling fully responsible for the movement of whichever finger moved. This strongly suggests that when they were subject to magnetic stimulation, participants were under the illusion that they were the sources of the decision to move one finger rather than the other.

It does seem possible to be mistaken in thinking that you are exercising your conscious will. Nonetheless, it appears that many of our behaviors are best explained by citing psychological phenomena. There is your aunt Hadida on her hands and knees behind a couch in the living room. Why? The behavior calls out for explanation. Merely citing neural causes might shed light on how she ended up in that location, but it will not make sense of why she is performing an action that seems prima facie odd. However, an explanation such as, "She had lost her bracelet, and thought it might be behind the couch," seems to be a candidate for accounting for what she is doing. It is hard to see, that is, that neural explanations can make sense of the goal-directed nature of our actions, while citing their origins in acts of consciously willing appears suited for the task.

Rumors of the death of conscious will are, I suggest, an exaggeration. Proponents of the adaptive unconscious are still within their rights to urge that conscious will has a smaller scope than many of us would like to believe. Given the wide range of automatic behavior that we have observed in this chapter, what emerges is that a good portion of our lives is carried on automatically. Conscious will still has a role to play, but that role is restricted to those cases in which we have to size up a novel situation and work out a reasonably complex strategy for handling it. Depending on what kind of life you lead, entire days may go by with little or no exercise of conscious will.

Implicit Attitudes

Many of us likely feel that we do not harbor attitudes that could be described as racist, sexist, homophobic, or discriminatory toward people with disabilities. After all, we take such attitudes to be morally objectionable, and if we introspect, we do not find ourselves harboring any such bigotry. However, even if we sincerely disavow any such attitudes available to introspection, we may still harbor them at the subconscious level. In fact, if the adaptive unconscious approach to such attitudes is correct, we may harbor bigoted attitudes in spite of sincerely rejecting bigotry! Why should we ascribe such unsavory views to people who sincerely and in good faith disavow them?

The reason is simply that for many of us, there is evidence in favor of such an ascription. Imagine an experiment that might support it. You are seated in a laboratory looking at a video screen. You are now told a story in which you are leaving a party and are starting to walk home. The screen depicts two different paths, one down a well-lit street, the other down a street that is dimly lit. Unbeknownst to you, before being shown these scenes, you were flashed an image of an African-American man's face for a very short period of time, indeed so short that you did not register it consciously. The question is whether this stimulation makes a difference for whether you are more likely to choose the well-lit or dimly lit street on your way home. In fact, after this subliminal stimulation, many subjects are more likely to choose the well-lit street than the dimly lit one, whereas if they had not received any such subliminal priming, they would have been equally likely to choose either street. A reasonable explanation of this choice seems to be that the subliminal stimulation makes subjects more anxious about their safety, which in turn explains why they choose the path that appears to be safer. Further, if that is so, then so long as we can also establish that a similar effect would not have been produced by subliminal priming of a Caucasian face, then the most likely conclusion is that seeing a black face activates anxiety in these subjects at the unconscious level.

If you can get online and have a few minutes to spare, you can assess the extent of your own implicit bias. Just go to https://implicit.harvard.edu/implicit/ to take one of the many tests that are available there. You can assess the extent of any implicit preference you may have for skin tone, sexuality, or gender, among other features. Just be forewarned: you may not like what the results of the test show you about yourself! Also, notice that if this or some other assessment shows that you harbor implicit bias, you have learned about an unconscious state of your own by third-personal or extrospective means. In addition, if you do harbor such unconscious states, their not being open to introspective access shows that they are subconscious rather than pre-conscious.

If you do find implicit bias within yourself, or learn of it in others, you might wonder where it could have come from. Perhaps earlier in your life you were, say, a racist and now have mended your ways. If that were so, you might explain the bias as being due to imperfect mending. But that explanation would seem not to apply to most people today. Another possibility is that simply by growing up exposed to media and other aspects of contemporary life, sexism, racism, and other biases will sink in whether you want them to or not. As a small child you might have watched movies and television shows in which the hero was a white male, while the women were subservient to them and the black characters were either villains or were morally ambiguous. Or consider some great cultural icons: the ceiling of the Sistine Chapel in the Vatican shows a white God giving life to a white Adam; the *Mona Lisa* was definitely not black, and Rodin's *The Thinker* tends to look like yet another white male. Further, as an adult you are exposed to ubiquitous advertising that tends to presuppose cultural stereotypes. As a result of a lifetime of stimulation, much of which happens at the periphery of conscious awareness, it should actually come as no surprise that you may harbor attitudes not comporting with your conscious, egalitarian views.

The natural next question is whether our implicit biases have any effects on our behavior. Some studies have offered striking, if discomfiting results. For instance, Bertrand et al. (2005) argue that a portion of racial discrimination in the real estate market is due to implicit bias.[7] Such a conclusion might be supported by an experiment of the following kind: send couples who are potential home buyers to a given realtor, making sure that the couples are alike on all relevant factors (income and education level, credit history, etc.) other than race. Then see if the realtor treats the white couple differently from the non-white couple. Given that the couples are alike in other relevant respects, the most plausible conclusion to draw is bias. If, further, the realtor disavows racist attitudes and may be presumed to be telling the truth, that would suggest that the best explanation of the realtor's behavior is that they harbor racist attitudes implicitly rather than explicitly. More broadly, as discussed in a review by Staats (2014), researchers have detected implicit bias in the way doctors prescribe medicine to their patients, hiring decisions by employers, sentencing decisions in courts of law, and in many other areas.

Suppose that you've visited the Project Implicit website and found some evidence of implicit bias in yourself. Is there anything you can do? This is a reasonable question, since harboring such biases could have implications for your behavior. I have no easy or general solutions to offer. However, there may be ways of remediating such biases in specific cases. For instance, as an educator I grade a good number of student papers each year. Just to be on the safe side, why not have students submit their papers anonymously, with only an identification number rather than their name on the title page? This way I will be more likely to be ignorant of their gender, race, ethnicity, and so on while assessing their work. Similarly, a realtor might create a database sorting former clients into broad categories based on both price range that the clients can afford, and the type of home they were seeking (free-standing or condo, urban, suburban, exurban, etc.). Once such categories are established, she can sort new clients into one of these categories and in the process be more likely to treat them broadly on a par with others she has served earlier regardless of their race, sexual orientation, and so on. Or you work in the Human Resources department of your corporation and want to help ensure that hiring and promotion decisions are driven by the skills of applicants instead of their gender, sexual orientation, body-type, and the like. A similar strategy to that of the realtor may be useful, centering around general benchmarks rather than your personal impressions of those seeking employment or promotion.

Conclusion

If recent theorizing under the banner of the adaptive unconscious is on the right track, then some unexpected implications follow about our ability to know ourselves and the value of doing so. First of all, some of what is said to be unconscious on this theory might instead occur on the periphery of consciousness. What is important for enabling it to proceed efficiently is not, however, whether it is unconscious or not, but that it is automatic. Further, the automaticity of these processes suggests that we will benefit from introspecting upon them (or learning about them extrospectively) only in special circumstances. A physician need feel no great need to examine the operations of the accounting firm to which she outsources her billing. She will likely benefit from doing so if either (a) she develops a curiosity about how accounting firms work, or (b) she has reason to suspect that something is amiss at this particular firm. So too, I might take an interest in, for instance, how language is processed or how faces are recognized. In that case, delving into the workings of the adaptive unconscious could be fascinating. Alternatively, I might have reason to think that something is amiss in my own adaptive unconscious. Remember our earlier mention of habits of the heart? Doubting that all of my emotional habits are serving me well, I might wonder, either on my own prompting or that of my therapist, why I continue to expect people I care about to abandon me abruptly; or why every time I succeed in one task I immediately think about other areas in which I am less successful, leaving no time to savor the success. But perhaps I can catch myself doing one of these things and try to redirect the relevant thoughts: "I did this; I'm happy about it, and should savor the moment. Worry about other challenges tomorrow." Or, "This person has never shown any tendency to abandon me. Why think they're about to ghost me now?"[8]

We may also appreciate an unexpected conclusion from our discussion of somatic markers. If A. Damasio's posit of such phenomena is correct, then we may learn about our own feelings by experiencing the external world. It is by looking (and otherwise sensing) outward (gazing at my email inbox, listening to the voice of an old friend, placing my hand on the knob of a door I am about to walk through) that I can detect the ways in which objects in my environment are somatically marked for me. That doorknob as I touch it might fill me with dread; I look upon that email subject line with excitement; I hear the voice of an old friend nostalgically, and so on. By attending to how these external objects strike me, I learn about how I feel. Thus if Damasio's hypothesis is on the right track, we can no longer expect to draw a clean line between introspection and extrospection. Instead, even looking outward can teach us about what is within.

Here is yet another implication of what we have learned in this chapter. Before reading it you may have known nothing of implicit bias. Now you know something about the phenomenon. What is more, if your choices and reactions to others have an impact on others' lives (that is, unless you are not a hermit who makes no use of social media), you also know that you may harbor implicit bias in spite of your sincere disavowal of bigotry of any kind. In that case, then I submit to you that you are under an obligation not just to yourself, but to others whose lives your choices may affect, to find out the extent and kind of your implicit bias; or barring that, at least to take measures to ensure that any such biases are relatively ineffective. Even though we generally do not become sick and carry contagious illness at will, if we are aware of our danger to others when afflicted with illness, we incur some obligation to protect them from our germs. So too, even though we do not invite implicit bias into our minds, unless we may be confident of its absence we bear some responsibility not to "infect" others with this particular kind of social disease.

Chapter Summary

- The theory of the adaptive unconscious offers to take up where psychoanalytic theory left off, while being more directly subject to experimental validation.
- Proponents of the adaptive unconscious do not engage in what we called (Chapter 4) epistemic hijinks, in that they do not accuse those who challenge their theory of Resistance.
- The theory of the adaptive unconscious concerns those cognitive systems that process information and solve problems without requiring conscious attention.
- A central concept for understanding the adaptive unconscious is that of automaticity, which pertains to psychological processes that run their course without requiring exertion on our part. In spite of this characterization, automatic processes are not entirely beyond our control.

- One well-known argument, due to T. Wilson, aiming to establish his "snowball on top of the iceberg" metaphor, is not persuasive.
- Somatic markers are another important dimension of the adaptive unconscious, although they may be conscious. Such markers guide rational decision making by presenting items of experience as having emotional significance.
- The psychological immune system is that aspect of the adaptive unconscious that enables us to respond resiliently to both negative and positive events. Our lack of awareness of this system (termed "immune neglect") leads us to overestimate how future events (both negative and positive) will affect us.
- Discovery of the adaptive unconscious has led some researchers to conclude that conscious will is an illusion. One general argument for this conclusion rests on a dubious premise. Other arguments, referring to specific discoveries in neuroscience, support a more refined view of the extent to which our conscious decisions make a difference for what we do.
- Implicit attitudes (including implicit bias as a special case) are types of bias that, if real, would not be open to introspection. One can harbor implicit bias while sincerely denying any such attitude. There are reasons to suppose that each of us has an obligation to determine whether she or he harbors implicit biases, and if so, to try to rectify them. The Implicit Association Test is open to anyone with an internet connection to discern whether they harbor implicit biases.
- The phenomenon of somatic markers blurs the distinction between introspection and extrospection. One can learn about oneself by experiencing things in one's environment.

Study Questions

1. What is the adaptive unconscious, and why is the concept of automaticity central to it?
2. Explain some main ways in which the theories of the adaptive unconscious and of the psychoanalytic unconscious differ.
3. Briefly describe experimental evidence that supports the posit of two of the three following phenomena: implicit learning, unconscious emotion, and unconscious goal-setting.
4. What is a somatic marker, and how might such a marker be an aid to decision making?
5. Is it possible for a society to use propaganda to modify its members' somatic markers? Please explain your answer.
6. What is the psychological immune system? How is it related to the concept of immune neglect?
7. Can a person be racist without harboring any racist attitudes on which he can introspect? Please explain your answer, being sure in the course

of doing so to explain the kind of empirical evidence that might be relevant to settling this question.

8. In light of what we have stablished about somatic markers, is it possible to learn about one's emotions by attending to objects of sensory experience? Please explain your answer.

Notes

1. Authors such as Epstein (1994) instead use the term "cognitive unconscious," but that is too narrow for our purposes, since we should be open to the possibility of non-cognitive—for instance affective—psychological states having a role to play in this new view of the unconscious.

2. Damasio suggests (1994, chapter 9) that societies can use such means as propaganda to modify our erstwhile somatic markers. If a government hopes to secure its power by marginalizing a minority group, for instance, it can encourage people to perceive members of that group as non-human—as vermin, for instance. In this way, once members of that group begin to be persecuted, what would normally have been experiences of watching these events with aversive somatic markers will now become unmarked, or even marked positively. Here, Damasio contends, is one way in which a society can be sick.

3. For further discussion of theories of consciousness, see D. Carmel and M. Sprevak (2015) "What Is Consciousness?" in M. Massimi et al. (eds.) *Philosophy and the Sciences for Everyone* (New York: Routledge), pp. 103–22.

4. B. Libet (1985) "Unconscious Cerebral Initiative and the Role of Conscious Will in Voluntary Action," *Behavioral and Brain Sciences*, vol. 8, pp. 529–66.

5. E. J. Sternberg (2010) *My Brain Made Me Do It: The Rise of Neuroscience and the Threat to Moral Responsibility* (Amherst, NY: Prometheus Books).

6. J. P. Brasil-Neto, A. Pascaul-Leone, J. Valls-Solé, L. G. Cohen, and M. Hallett (1992) "Focal Transcranial Magnetic Stimulation and Response Bias in a Forced-Choice Task," *Journal of Neurology, Neurosurgery, and Psychiatry*, vol. 55, pp. 964–6.

7. M. Bertrand, D. Chugh, and S. Mullainathan (2005) "Implicit Discrimination," *American Economic Review*, vol. 95, pp. 94–8.

8. An extensive discussion of such matters is in T. Wilson (2011) *Redirect: Changing the Stories We Live By* (New York: Little, Brown).

Introductory Further Readings

Carmel, D. and M. Sprevak. (2015) 'What Is Consciousness?' in M. Massimi et al. (eds.) *Philosophy and the Sciences for Everyone* (New York: Routledge), pp. 103–22. Accessible, brief discussion of both philosophical and scientific issues associated with consciousness.

Damasio, A. (1994) *Descartes' Error: Emotion, Reason, and the Human Brain* (New York: Penguin). Classic discussion from a neuroscientist of the role of emotion in decision making.

Kane, R. (2005) *A Contemporary Introduction to Free Will* (New York: Oxford University Press). Influential and highly accessible discussion of the central issues in the problem of free will.

Mele, A. (2009) *Effective Intentions: The Power of Conscious Will* (Oxford: Oxford University Press). A detailed discussion by a philosopher of the implications of Libet's and other experiments.

Nahmias, E. (2014) 'Is Free Will an Illusion? Confronting Challenges from the Modern Mind Sciences,' in W. Sinnott-Armstrong (ed.) *Moral Psychology, Vol 4: Freedom and Responsibility* (Cambridge, MA: MIT Press), pp. 1–26. Careful philosophical treatment of the threat posed by recent developments in neuroscience for our conception of freedom of will.

Staats, C. (2014) *State of the Science: Implicit Bias Review 2014*, Kirwan Institute, Ohio State University. (http://cte.virginia.edu/wp-content/uploads/2016/01/2014-implicit-bias_pp.70-73.pdf). Useful literature survey on implicit bias.

Wegner, D., and T. Wheatley (1999) 'Apparent Mental Causation: Sources of the Experience of Will,' *American Psychologist*, vol. 54, pp. 80–92. Intriguing discussion of human behavior that assumes that conscious decision-making plays no role in producing our behavior.

Wilson, T. (2002) *Strangers to Ourselves: Discovering the Adaptive Unconscious* (Cambridge, MA: Harvard University Press). Extended defense of the adaptive unconscious, including discussion of the relative merits of this approach to that of psychoanalysis.

Advanced Further Readings

Bargh, J., A. Lee-Chai, K. Barndollar, P. Gollwitzer, and R. Trötschel. (2001) 'The Automated Will: Nonconscious Activation and Pursuit of Behavioral Goals,' *Journal of Personality and Social Psychology*, vol. 81, pp. 1014–27. Experimental investigation of unconscious influences on behavior.

Brownstein, M. and J. Saul (eds.). (2016) *Implicit Bias and Philosophy*, Vols. I and II (Oxford: Oxford University Press). Essays by psychologists and philosophers on the nature and implications of implicit bias.

Claparède, E. (1911/1951) 'Recognition and "Me-Ness," ' in D. Rapaport (ed.) *Organization and Pathology of Thought* (New York: Columbia University Press), pp. 58–75. Classic study of unconscious learning.

Epstein, S. (1994) 'Integration of the Cognitive and Psychodynamic Unconscious,' *American Psychologist*, vol. 49, pp. 709–24. An early defense of what we now call the adaptive unconscious.

Halpern, J., and R. Arnold (2008) 'Affective Forecasting: An Unrecognized Challenge in Making Serious Health Decisions,' *Journal of General Internal Medicine*, vol. 23, pp. 1708–1712. Important study of the implications of affective forecasting for difficult health care decisions.

Hofmann, W. and T. Wilson. (2010) 'Consciousness, Introspection, and the Adaptive Unconscious,' in B. Gawronski and B. Payne (eds.) *Handbook of Implicit Social Cognition* (New York: Guilford Press), pp. 197–215. Useful discussion of the relation of the three concepts mentioned in the article title.

Levy, N. (2016) 'Implicit Bias and Moral Responsibility: Probing the Data,' *Philosophy and Phenomenological Research*, vol. 94, pp. 3–26. An empirically well-informed discussion of the question whether we are morally responsible for modifying our implicit biases.

Reber, A. (1989) 'Implicit Learning and Tacit Knowledge,' *Journal of Experimental Psychology: General*, vol. 118, pp. 219–35. Wide-ranging survey of multiple sources of experimental evidence supporting the phenomenon of implicit learning.

Wilson, T. (2011) *Redirect: Changing the Stories We Live By* (New York: Little, Brown). Discussion, from the point of view of the adaptive unconscious, of various ways in which behavior can be modified in light of these new experimental findings.

Wilson, T. and D. Gilbert. (2005) 'Affective Forecasting: Knowing What to Want,' *Current Directions in Psychological Science*, vol. 14, pp. 131–4. Influential discussion of affective forecasting, including discussion of the concept of immune neglect.

Zemack-Rugar, Y., J. Bettman, and G. Fitzsimons. (2007) 'The Effects of Non-Consciously Priming Emotion Concepts on Behavior,' *Journal of Personality and Social Psychology*, vol. 93, pp. 927–39. Experimental demonstration of unconscious methods of activating emotional responses.

Internet Resources

Gennaro, R. (n.d.) 'Consciousness,' in J. Feiser and B. Dowden (eds.) *Internet Encyclopedia of Philosophy* (www.iep.utm.edu/consciou/). Accessible introductory discussion of philosophical issues surrounding consciousness.

Project Implicit (https://implicit.harvard.edu/implicit/). Anyone may visit this website and choose one of the many tests it contains to detect implicit bias.

6 Self-Misleading, Empathy, and Humility

Some Varieties of Self-Deception

In English-speaking philosophy over the last several decades, self-deception has been treated as a kind of logical puzzle: common sense would suggest that we seem to be quite capable of self-deception, but would not truly deceiving yourself mean that you believe something that you know not to be true? If so, one might ask, how is that so much as possible? If you know something, you must also believe it. But then, if there is some proposition A that you know, then you must also believe A. And then, how could you also not believe it? Or perhaps you believe that A is true and believe that A is also not true? But that seems like a case in which you have contradicted yourself, not one in which you've deceived yourself.

Anglophone philosophers have devised a number of theories that try to preserve the puzzling nature of self-deception without turning it into sheer self-contradiction. However, our purposes are not well served by exploring those theories in any detail. Instead our focus will be on activities that are less extreme than the "believing something you know not to be true" variety. To mark the distinction I shall call them *self-misleading* instead of self-deception. While perhaps less theoretically exciting for the philosopher, I contend that cases of self-misleading are more pertinent to the sorts of epistemic troubles we get into with ourselves in our daily lives. The cases below involve varying degrees of agency, that is, they differ on the extent to which they involve an active doing or allowing on our part.

Cherry-picking the evidence: I firmly believe that I am lactose-intolerant, based on my experience of drinking a large milkshake and feeling ill soon thereafter. Others have pointed out to me that something else besides the milk in that shake might have made me sick, but I insist that it was the milk, and continue to consume only lactose-free products.

Wishful thinking: I go to a sporting goods store and an expensive set of technical rock climbing gear catches my eye: ropes, shoes, Camalots, belay devices, helmet, ropes, and so forth. In little time I convince myself that owning these things will motivate me to get over my fear of rock climbing and take up the sport, and I buy them. Months pass as these unused items collect dust in the corner of my living room.

Rationalizing after the fact: I just ate a whole lot more nachos than I needed to or should have. Afterwards I say to myself, "I must have been hungrier than I thought!" Sometimes, of course, that description is quite true. In this case, I was not in fact unusually hungry, but instead I have been using my behavior as an indication of the extent of my previous hunger.

Procrastinating with busywork: I put off working on a hard problem by obsessing over small details that, as I work through them, seem urgent. As a result I don't leave enough time for the more difficult problem, on which I never make much progress. I may however been telling myself all along that I've been working on the details in order to attack the hard problem.

Humblebragging: It is not uncommon to hear someone offering what on the surface is a complaint, but that, on further reflection, seems to be designed to enable them to flaunt something they are proud of. I might complain about how I can't decide among all these high-profile speaking invitations I have received for the same calendar date. (*Subtext*: Look at all the enviable speaking invitations I've received!) Or I might bemoan the fact that I cannot take my Newfoundland dog out in public because everyone wants to stop to pet her. (*Subtext*: What a beautiful dog I have!) What is important for our purposes is that in cases like these, I might not be aware of the fact that I am attempting to flaunt something of which I am proud. Further, this desire to flaunt might also be in service of a desire to make you jealous; here too I may not be aware of this motive.

Perfectionism: Being a perfectionist might sound simply like a way of having high standards. However, perfectionism may also be a way of duping oneself into mediocrity. If, as is the case with nearly every project, I have to get something done by a certain time, and I have merely normal or above-average abilities, then perfection will be unattainable. A mediocre product is more likely.

In these cases it is not just that the person is mistaken about herself, either by failing to recognize a psychological characteristic that she has, or by ascribing to herself a psychological characteristic that she lacks. Rather, what unites these cases seems to be that they all involve an *ulterior motive*: in the cherrypicking case, I seem to have a desire to reach this self-diagnosis (perhaps because lactose intolerance is so trendy), in the wishful thinking case I would seem to want to be the sort of person who can use technical skills to climb a sheer rock face; in the rationalizing case, of course, those nachos are very good, and so forth. While the above six cases are simply anecdotes I have collected from my own actions and my observation of others, I submit that at least the interesting cases in which we mislead ourselves are ones in which we have an ulterior motive to do so. Further, that ulterior motive can be brought up into conscious awareness if we make an effort to spot it. The process, however, may not be pleasant.

Accordingly, rather than attempting to develop a general account of how cases of self-misleading work, and relate to one another, it will be enough for now to recognize that in each one of them, if a good friend could hear what we say to ourselves when engaged in that activity, and knew the facts of the situation, she might challenge our behavior or attitudes. For the case of procrastinating with busywork, for instance, she might point out that given the deadline I am up against, working out all these details is sure to make me get little done on the harder task. Likewise, a friend might call me out for bragging even though what I said, at the time I said it, only felt like a complaint. No doubt, we do sometimes fool our friends. However, part of what it is to be a friend is to resist the temptation to be misled by others' smokescreens. A good friendship will survive the confrontation that such resistance (or even Resistance!) might require. That may be in part because friends are generally adept at empathizing with one another.

What Is Empathy and Why Does It Matter?

We are commonly reminded of the importance of empathizing with other people. However, it is not often made clear what this activity involves and why it is worth engaging in. To make progress on the former question, let us first distinguish between emotional contagion and empathy. "Emotional contagion" refers to the process by which we "catch" the emotions of those around us. I can easily be seized with anger if I am surrounded by angry people, and being in a room full of melancholy people can cause that mood to rub off on me as well. Emotional contagion probably has a long evolutionary history. Humans did not evolve from any currently existing great apes such as chimpanzees. Instead, we share a common evolutionary ancestor with them. It is nevertheless suggestive that one can easily find video clips of members of one troop of chimpanzees working themselves into a murderous frenzy as they prepare to raid the territory of another troop.

Emotional contagion is not, however, empathy. One necessary condition for empathy is that one direct one's attention toward another and feel some concern for them or otherwise take an interest in their well-being. However, one can undergo emotional contagion without feeling concern for others or taking an interest in their welfare. For instance, I might get caught up in the anger of those around me without caring about them or taking the least interest in their well-being.

Empathy is also distinct from both sympathy and compassion. I can be sympathetic with someone else by feeling or showing some concern for them. If I am a nurse, for instance, I might show sympathy and compassion for someone suffering from an overdose of heroin. Treating them kindly, doing all I can to minimize their suffering and help them to recover, would seem to be enough to show them sympathy and/or compassion toward them. However, here too we do not yet have empathy. Instead, unlike emotional contagion and sympathy, empathy involves—to speak metaphorically—putting oneself in the shoes of another. Unpacking that metaphor, we might suggest that empathy requires imagining one's way into another's emotional situation. This might not be easy, and we may in some cases be convinced that we are empathizing with someone when it is doubtful that we are. (I doubt, for instance, that I can empathize with someone from a radically different culture from my own without a great deal of work, which at the very least would require learning about their culture's history and practices.) Instead, to empathize with someone I must imagine feeling something close to what they are feeling or otherwise undergoing psychologically. (Although we normally think of empathy as directed toward someone who is suffering, I see no in-principle bar to empathizing with someone to whom something good has happened. I see no reason, that is, why we cannot empathize with a friend who has married the partner of her dreams, or with someone who has received the promotion he had been seeking for many years.)

Suppose you have just lost a loved one to cancer and are now grieving. How might I empathize with you? I may, but need not grieve along with you in order to do so. Instead, one way to empathize with you would be to call upon my own prior experience with grief (assuming I have some such experience) and use that as a key to imagine my way into your situation. I recall, from my past experience of grieving, such experiences as these: wishing I could get the loved one back; carrying on imaginary conversations with her; being strongly affected by things that remind me of her, such as articles of clothing, distinctive phrases she would use, or music she liked. I also recall finding myself breaking into tears at unexpected moments, and so on. Putting these together I can form a sense of what you might be going through, and on *that* basis be in a better positon to be helpful to you if you call upon me for aid.

Empathy, then, requires imagining one's way into another's situation, and taking an interest in their well-being. Drawing on one's own experience with an emotion (grief, disappointment, abandonment, unexpected success), one can use that as a basis, while making appropriate modifications, to get a sense of another's situation, and be prepared to offer help or support accordingly. Some people might find empathizing more natural than do others. For those who do find empathizing natural, nothing in our account of the phenomenon rules out the possibility of empathizing in a way that is automatic (in the sense of this term we developed in Chapter 5). That is, just as I might automatically form a mental picture of the location of a ball that has rolled behind a bush, so too, on the basis of my own experience with a particular emotion, I might automatically imagine what your situation is like when you undergo that emotion.

It may appear from what we have said so far that the range of emotions one can empathize with will be restricted to the emotions one has oneself experienced. However, I suspect that part of what we can get out of works of art such as literature, film, drama, music, photography, and even painting are tools that we may use for empathetic engagement with others. Green (2008, 2010, 2016) has argued that skilled novelists can give readers a sense of what the emotions are like that their characters undergo. The author Jane Hamilton, for instance, in her novel *A Map of the World* gives us a sense of what it feels like to be ostracized by others. I suspect that if we read carefully and take the characterizations of this novel to heart, we can, first, learn what ostracism feels like, and then, on that basis, empathize with someone who is feeling ostracized without ever feeling or having felt that emotion ourselves. As a first step, we might empathize with the character in the novel who is feeling ostracized; then, on that basis we might be able to empathize with real people who are undergoing similar emotions.

Empathy, then, can mobilize one's own emotional experience, as well as what one can learn about the contour of such emotions through reading good literature, in order to help us understand what others are going through. This can be of value in helping us to understand others from different walks of life and of different points of view. Someone who was born and raised in comfortable material circumstances might have trouble understanding why anyone would steal, use drugs, or lack the energy or confidence to look for work. Reading a novel about someone in this situation, or watching a film such as *Winter's Bone* (2010, directed by Debra Granik) can take that person some of the distance toward understanding the hopeless desperation that can afflict those experiencing chronic poverty. So too, one who has had limited contact with members of the LGBQT community might find incomprehensible, and perhaps even repulsive the idea of taking a romantic interest in a member of the same sex. Lyrics from a song, a series of photographs, or lines of poetry may, however, all help that person to appreciate what it feels like to be attracted to someone as a person regardless of their gender identification. Even if one persists in experiencing feelings of heterosexual attraction only, one will still be better equipped to appreciate that others of different orientation are not, just by virtue of that difference, either evil or mentally ill.

When Reasonable People Differ

So far we have considered what one might term "affective empathy", by which we imagine our way into another's affective situation, be it an emotion or a mood. However, the value of empathy in helping us to bridge gaps created by different life experiences, orientations, and personalities is not limited to enabling us to show concern for others' emotions and moods. It also enables us to appreciate how another person might react differently to the same information that you have access to. Hence although we have spoken so far about empathizing with someone's affective situation, nothing in the concept rules out the possibility of empathizing with someone's epistemic situation. What might such *cognitive empathy* consist in?

Here is an illustration. I might hear someone remark that because it has been quite a while since there has been a major earthquake in the area where she lives, "we're due for a big one." This attitude presupposes that an area's recent history of earthquakes may be used as a predictor for whether an earthquake is likely to happen soon. (Similar assumptions may support analogous predictions about impending blizzards, tornadoes, lightning strikes, and so on.) That is a tempting assumption, although one that I know to have little support. (It is only if we have independent reason to think that pressure is building on the overlapping plates that make up the earth's crust in the area that we should take this assumption to be justified.) Barring that support, I would not accept the claim that we're due for a big earthquake simply because we have not had one for a while.

In spite of not accepting this claim, I can surely understand the attitude that motivates it. The idea that nature has a balance sheet that needs occasionally to be corrected is a tempting one, not least because it makes us feel that the world around us behaves in an orderly and intelligible manner. With these thoughts in mind, I can also empathize with someone who believes that we are due for an earthquake soon. I can, that is, imagine myself believing what they do about how nature operates and drawing conclusions from this imagined point of view. What is more, if I am careful, I can do this while also keeping in mind that both this conclusion and the view of nature supporting it are mistaken. Likewise, recall our discussion in Chapter 1 of some slogans one hears in everyday life ("If it makes you happy, it can't be that bad," "Everything happens for a reason," and "Better safe than sorry") that are not, under close scrutiny, very plausible. Here too one can see why these slogans might be attractive at first glance, and why someone might accept one or more of them. That understanding might enable able to cognitively empathize with such a person while still disagreeing with them, and without condescending to them.

Cognitive empathy, then, can help us to understand those with whom we disagree even when we are confident that they are mistaken. Such an attitude promotes tolerance with those with whom we differ. It also helps us to confront situations in which people might disagree on a matter in which neither one seems to have compelling reason for preferring her own view to that of the other. Suppose that you and a friend (who is more or less on the same level as you in terms of education and overall intelligence) find that you have opposed views about a difficult question, such as the reason for the extinction of the dinosaurs, the causes of the dramatic spike in cancer rates in the last century, or the issue of which activities and lifestyles are most likely to stave off the onset of Alzheimer's disease. Further discussion reveals that neither of you is missing information that the other has, and neither of you can find an obvious flaw in the other's reasoning.

The foregoing are examples of the phenomenon that philosophers interested in the nature of knowledge call the problem of *peer disagreement*. What is the, or at least a, reasonable response to such an impasse? One approach is to dig in your heels and say that the other person is wrong: he must have made a mistake in his reasoning somewhere. To speak with Descartes, on this approach you might accuse your friend of failing to use clear and distinct perception.

This attitude seems however, to be a form of hubris. After all, could not your friend accuse you of precisely the same thing? More generally, if your conclusion from the data is more accurate than your friend's, it cannot be due *merely* to the fact that it is your conclusion. For we've assumed that you and your friend are on a par in terms of overall smarts and expertise. (Matters would be different if one of you were an expert in the area in question, or were significantly more adept than the other in processing and analyzing information.) Another attitude seems to be more reasonable, namely that at least one of you must be mistaken, but we are not yet in a position to discern who that might be. Instead we just need to keep gathering more evidence and analyzing it carefully to see which of our two views will be ruled out. (I say "at least" because it may be that you are both wrong: perhaps there is a third, better answer that neither of you has considered thus far.)

We may of course never be so fortunate as to get to the bottom of things: war might break out, one of us might pass away, or research on the issue in question might come to a halt due to a dramatic reduction in institutional funding. Until one of those things happens, however, a reasonable lesson to draw from the fact that an epistemic peer disagrees with me over a matter on which I had a firm view, is to revise the firmness of that view. Perhaps my position has been that the spike in cancer rates over the last century is due to the prevalence of plastics in our food supply. That might be consistent with, and even suggested by, the available evidence. However, the fact that "reasonable people can disagree" on this issue shows that my conclusion is one of at least two such views on the matter that it is rational to hold; someone else might explain cancer rates as due to greater sun exposure among the population, greater consumption of saturated fats, and the like. Unless I can find some ground for preferring my own view other than the fact that it is mine, it would seem reasonable to moderate my commitment to that view. How might I do that? One way is to revise my belief (and corresponding statements) so that they are now *conjectures*. This attitude involves working with an idea that you think has some, but not conclusive support, in the hope of discovering such support as new evidence comes in or as we sharpen our understanding of the evidence that we already have. One who conjectures some proposition does not claim to know that proposition, but merely indicates that we have some reason to believe it. Further, knowing that my epistemic peer has made a different conjecture to explain the same evidence does not undermine or directly challenge my own. Instead we may just shake hands and say, "May the best theory win!"

Faced, then, with cases of peer disagreement, I suggest that a reasonable course is to downgrade our convictions to the level of conjectures. One benefit of this process is that it enables us to exercise our capacity for cognitive empathy: as you consider the alternative conjecture that your epistemic peer contemplates, you likely will be able to imagine your way into how they might have arrived at the conjecture they have. Perhaps you will even come over to their side. Even if you do not do so, however, you are likely to be less dogmatic with your own point of view and more able to see the same data through different lenses.

Intellectual and Other Forms of Humility

Thus far in this chapter we have considered some ways in which we are prone to mislead ourselves, often on the basis of motives that are difficult to acknowledge. We have also examined empathy and seen that it involves imagining one's way into another's affective situation, while also taking some concern for their well-being. This affective form of empathy may be distinguished from cognitive empathy, by which we imagine ourselves into another's epistemic situation.

Doing so may prepare us to respond appropriately to cases of peer disagreement by revising our convictions into conjectures, or otherwise take a step away from those convictions. All these processes may be seen as calling upon us to be humble about the extent of our knowledge of others and of the world around us.

We are naturally prone to what psychologists call the Fundamental Attribution Error (FAE): when something goes well for me, I deserve the credit, while when something does not go well for me, the rest of the world is to blame! For instance, when you are driving and another driver cuts you off, that person is an utter jerk; while if you cut someone else off, that is simply due to the fact that you're in a hurry, did not see them, and so forth. Taking the FAE to heart, that is, admitting that I am just as prone to this kind of error as is anyone else, is difficult, even disturbing. I would like to think that I am a decent judge of the reasons why things happen and of who is responsible for those events; yet the FAE should at least lead me to suspect that I overestimate my astuteness in this matter. In light of such considerations, Whitcomb et al. (2017) advocate a characterization of intellectual humility as *owning up to one's own limitations*. These come in two forms: the first concerns those distorting processes to which most of us are prone, such as FAE. The second concerns awareness of any idiosyncratic limitations: perhaps I am vain about particular issues, and have a blind spot about others. Acknowledging both generic and idiosyncratic limitations puts me in a position to challenge my first thoughts about how to solve problems and answer questions with such words as, "Why do I think that? What if someone were to disagree—could I win them over."

A more general characterization of what I am suggesting here is as follows. If I hold an opinion, one that I am prepared to assert and thereby represent myself as knowing to be true, intellectual humility bids me to ask: have I looked at the available evidence carefully, and if someone else were to do the same, would they come to a similar conclusion? If I have reason for doubting that the answer to this latter question is "Yes," I should revise my view, either by retracting it outright or downgrading it to a conjecture or even an educated guess. This is all because *reasons are inherently general*: if I have good reasons for a position, I should be able to present those reasons to someone else and bring them over to my side without use of epistemic hijinks. If I have doubts about doing so, rationality bids me to revise my position.

The point generalizes to certain emotions. Many emotions are inherently evaluative: anger at someone tends to cast them as having wronged you, while embarrassment tends to represent its owner as having transgressed a social norm. As such, certain emotions might be more or less *apt*. I might challenge someone else's emotion by remarking, "Your anger is completely out of proportion to what that other person did," or "You've got no need to feel embarrassed; these things happen all the time and are no big deal." *Affective* humility, accordingly, bids us to ask ourselves when in the grip of an emotion, whether someone else in the same situation would respond similarly, and if not, why not? Unlike reasons for beliefs, differences in personality might bring about different emotional responses (some of us are more irascible than others, and some are more easily embarrassed than others). However, if I can imagine another person with roughly congruent character traits to mine, that might help me to consider whether my emotional response to the current situation is the, or at least an, apt one. More often than we might expect, we will have trouble convincing ourselves that the answer is a resounding "Yes."

You will have noticed that one who cultivates intellectual or affective humility makes an effort to stand outside herself: in recognizing that her view is one among many that might be held on a certain manner, she is implicitly acknowledging that other viewpoints than her own are not only possible, but may well be reasonable. Similarly, one who empathizes with another adopts a different point of view by imagining her way into the other's shoes. In imagining how they feel or think, I thereby imagine seeing things as they do: if I am successful in empathizing with the experience of a racial or ethnic minority, for instance, I have some sense of what it feels like to be profiled or harassed by the police, or being the subject of micro-aggressions from people who think they're being funny or clever.

A striking implication follows from both the practice of intellectual or affective humility, as well as that of empathizing, namely that these activities provide an opportunity to look at ourselves from an external vantage point. By empathizing with someone who is the victim of racism, for instance, I come to appreciate how profoundly I take for granted that police are not likely to harass me when I drive my car, or that shopkeepers in stores I enter will not trail behind me expecting to catch me shoplifting. By empathizing with someone who is experiencing grief, I can better appreciate how much my own loss in the past affected me. So too, by empathizing with someone's satisfaction over a challenging job well done, I can better appreciate the value I attach to pushing against my own limitations.

A recent development in research on self-knowledge concerns *self-distancing*, or that process by which we view ourselves from an external perspective such as when Advika thinks, "Why did this happen to Advika and how should she respond," in contrast to the self-immersed, "Why did this happen to me, and how should I respond?" According to this line of inquiry, the perspective of a "fly on the wall" helps us to acknowledge our foibles, our blindspots, and our tendency to overestimate ourselves (Kross and Grossmann 2011). This perspective also helps to prevent out ruminating when faced with emotionally challenging situations (Kross and Ayduk, 2011). Researchers studying self-distancing have found that this approach results in subjects reporting less distress in response to emotional challenges than do those who self-immerse, and such subjects tend to recover from the challenge in a shorter time. Research also suggests that the self-distancing approach benefits the psychological health of those diagnosed with clinical depression as well as those diagnosed with bipolar disorder (Kross and Ayduk, 2011).

If this work on the value of self-distancing is on the right track, then it is yet more evidence that what we called in earlier chapters the third-personal, or extrospective approach to the self, is conducive to wisdom—perhaps even more than introspection. In fact, we now see that empathizing, because it supports self-distancing, has the unexpected benefit of being helpful for the empathiz*er* and not just to the one with whom she is empath*izing*.

Chapter Summary

- Self-deception as here understood is a philosopher's puzzle that is not clearly germane to everyday concerns. By contrast, we regularly *mislead* ourselves, and such behavior is often motivated by a desire that we have difficulty acknowledging, rather than just the commission of an error about the causes of our behavior.
- Friends and others concerned with our well-being often try to empathize with our tendency to self-mislead, as a first step in helping us to do better.
- Empathy is distinct from emotional contagion, as well as from sympathy and compassion. The former require imagining one's way into the psychic situation of another.
- Empathizing with another does not require literally sharing their emotion; one may instead draw upon one's experience with that emotion.
- More controversially, it may also be that works of art such as fiction enable us to empathize with those emotions that we have never experienced.
- Empathy is not limited to imagining another's emotional situation; it also seems to permit imagining one's way into another's epistemic situation. Such cognitive empathy helps equip us to respond appropriately to cases of peer disagreement. Exercise of cognitive empathy helps us to see the limitations of our own viewpoints, and can help us to revise our beliefs into conjectures.
- Intellectual humility, here understood as acknowledging our own epistemic limitations, also requires awareness of common reasoning mistakes such as the Fundamental Attribution Error. We may also understand what it would mean to exercise affective humility.

Study Questions

1. What is the difference between self-deception and self-misleading? Please illustrate your answer with an example of misleading oneself. (If possible, try to devise an example other than those discussed in Section 2.)
2. What is emotional contagion? Why might it be thought that groups of animals (humans included) might gain a survival advantage from being disposed to emotional contagion?
3. What is empathy, as that notion has been characterized here. In your answer, it will be helpful to explain the differences among empathy, emotional contagion, and sympathy.
4. Please explain the difference between affective empathy and cognitive empathy. Next, recalling our discussion in Chapter 4 of the three main kind of mental states, might a third kind of empathy not be covered by the above two? Please explain your answer.

5.   Have you ever felt that reading a novel or short story enabled you to empathize with someone's emotion, even though you've never felt that emotion yourself? If so, please explain your answer. If not, is there an emotion that you'd like to be able to empathize with that a good novel might open up for you? Here too, please explain your answer.
6.   What is the problem of peer disagreement? Why might someone deny that the best response to such a situation is to dig in one's heels and insist that one is right? What might a more constructive response be?
7.   Please explain the concept of intellectual humility. Might there also be a phenomenon of affective humility? Please explain your answer.
8.   Might empathizing with others be conducive to self-knowledge? Please explain your answer.

Introductory Further Reading

Coplan, A. and P. Goldie (eds.). (2011) *Empathy: Philosophical and Psychological Perspectives* (Oxford: Oxford University Press). A collection of state of the art essays by philosophers and psychologists on empathy.

Green, M. (2008) 'Empathy, Expression, and What Artworks Have to Teach,' in G. Hagberg (ed.) *Art and Ethical Criticism* (Oxford: Blackwell), pp. 95–122. Discusses the nature of empathy, its relation to emotional expression, and connection of these two to the power of literature to teach us things.

———. (2010) 'How and What Can We Learn From Literature?' in G. Hagberg and W. Jost (eds.) *The Blackwell Companion to the Philosophy of Literature* (Hoboken, NJ: Wiley-Blackwell), pp. 350–66. Offers a view of literary of fiction as a source of knowledge, including knowledge of how someone in a dramatically different position from one's own might experience their world.

———. (2016) 'Learning to Be Good (or Bad) in (or Through) Literature,' in G. Hagberg (ed.) *Fictional Characters, Real Problems: The Search for Ethical Content in Literature* (Oxford: Oxford University Press), pp. 282–304. Argues that engagement with fictional characters can help us learn to empathize with real people, with the proviso that such an activity is not inherently one that makes us better people.

Hatfield, E., J. Cacciopo, and R. Rapson. (1993) *Emotional Contagion* (Cambridge: Cambridge University Press). The most comprehensive treatment of the phenomenon available. Although dense with discussion of experimental results, the book is highly readable.

Matheson, J. (2015) 'Disagreement and Epistemic Peers,' in D. Pritchard (ed.) *Oxford Handbooks Online*. Useful general introduction to the phenomenon of peer disagreement.

Advanced Further Reading

Andrews, P. (2001) 'The Psychology of Social Chess and the Evolution of Attribution Mechanisms: Explaining the Fundamental Attribution Error,' *Evolution and Human Behavior*, vol. 22, pp. 11–29. Offers an evolutionary explanation of FAE emphasizing the role of Theory of Mind as a driver of this process.

Decety, J. (ed.). (2014) *Empathy: From Bench to Bedside* (Cambridge, MA: MIT Press). A collection of essays examining empathy from the perspectives of social neuroscience, mammalian neural evolution, and clinical practice.

———, and O. Ayduk (2011) Making Meaning out of Negative Experiences by Self-Distancing,' *Current Directions in Psychological Science*, vol. 20, pp. 187–191. Compelling overview of research concerned with ways in which self-distancing can support a constructive response to an emotionally challenging situation.

Kross, E., and Grossmann, I. (2011) 'Boosting Wisdom: Distance from the Self Enhances Wise Reasoning, Attitudes, and Behavior,' *Journal of Experimental Psychology: General*. Vol. 141, pp. 43–48. Experimental study supporting the view that self-distancing is conducive to subjects making wise choices.

Whitcomb, D., H. Battaly, J. Baehr, and D. Howard-Snyder. (2017) 'Intellectual Humility: Owning Our Limitations,' *Philosophy and Phenomenological Research*, vol. 94, pp. 509–39. Carefully argued defense of a notion of intellectual humility focusing on acknowledging one's own limitations. Contains critical discussion of alternative conceptions of intellectual humility.

Internet Resources

Steuber, K. 'Empathy,' in E. Zalta (ed.) *The Stanford Encyclopedia of Philosophy*. Excellent overview of the topic of empathy, including discussion of its historical roots (https://plato.stanford.edu/entries/empathy/).

7 Persons
Some Western Approaches

Chapter Summary

One apparently fundamental constituent of self-knowledge is an appreciation of one's status as a person as opposed to a mere hunk of matter or flesh. This topic is the focus of the present chapter. Personal identity breaks down into synchronic (What is it for an entity at a particular time to be a person?) and diachronic (What is it for one "person-stage" to be a stage of one and the same person as another person-stage existing at another time?) questions. We will consider some well-known accounts of synchronic identity from both the dualist and materialist traditions. We will next discuss approaches to diachronic personal identity, the best known of which is John Locke's which emphasizes memories linking one person-stage to another prior to it. We will consider challenges to the Lockean view and consider whether it can be refined to accommodate them. We will also discuss challenges to Locke involving the possibility of "uploading" one's memories onto a server, as well as those concerning person-fission. Next we will sketch a view of diachronic identity for which bodily continuity is essential, but which will carry some surprising consequences if it is true.

Personhood and Moral Standing

In our conversation thus far we have taken for granted the assumption that each us is a person, or a self. Our focus has been on the questions whether it is possible to know about this self, and if so, how far that knowledge reaches and the value of such knowledge. In this final section of the book—comprising this and the next chapter—we will step back from that assumption to consider the strength of the posit of a definite self—of a thing that might exist at a time and persist through time.

I shall treat selves and persons as the same things. Thus while we might say that a laptop computer needs to restart itself, or that the moth is trying to camouflage itself among the tree's leaves to avoid being eaten, most of us do not think of either the computer or the moth as selves in the sense in which that term will be used here. Instead, for our purposes, being (or having) a self is the same as being a person. But what is that? To get a feel for the difficulty of this question, consider this story. In the fall of 2004, anthropologists working on the Indonesian island of Flores discovered skeletal remains of a three-foot-tall, flat-faced, bipedal hominid that had inhabited the area as recently as 12,000 years ago. This hominid was strikingly different from other well-known species such as *Homo habilis* and *Homo erectus*, and it has been named *Homo flore-siensis. Floresiensis'* skeletal remains were found in caves, together with stone tools of some intricacy as well as evidence of fire-making and of the hunting of large game. This discovery sparked a lively debate in the press and popular scientific publications concerning the status of these creatures. For instance, the popular science writer Desmond Morris asked, if we were to come upon a tribe of these creatures living today, should we treat them as advanced apes or as a form of human being?[1] Morris raises a good question, but his question is a bit out of focus. The category "human being" is a biological one, and *Homo erectus, Homo sapiens*, and *Homo floresiensis* all belong in it. However, we cannot simply assume that being a *human being* and being a *person* are the same thing. The former is a biological category, like the property of using photosynthesis for energy, or being an invertebrate. Such properties are not inherently connected to a creature's moral standing. By contrast, the category of being a person is, at least in part, a moral one. If *Homo floresiensis* is a person, then if we were to encounter one now we would be encountering a creature that has a moral status different in kind from a cat or a horse. For instance, while killing a cat might be morally wrong, it is not murder; by contrast, if *floresiensis* is a person, then killing it (unless we do so under extenuating conditions such as self-defense) certainly is.

Perhaps one can be a human being without being a person. If you suffer a terrible accident resulting in such grave brain damage that you enter an irretrievably vegetative state, then perhaps you cease to be a person while remaining a human being. Others hold that infants are human beings but not (yet) persons. It may also be possible to be a person without being a human being. From our discussion of Chapter 3, you can easily imagine why someone might hold that a sufficiently sophisticated computer could be a person without being a human being. Or again, one can imagine encountering a race of advanced aliens who, in spite of not being biologically like us at all, are persons but not human beings.

Since we cannot just assume that, like that of being a human being, being a person is a biological category, it does not seem that we can settle what a person is by looking through a microscope or excavating a prehistoric hearth. So how else might we go about settling the question, what counts as a person? Another tempting approach might be to settle it by our decision how to use the word "person." Perhaps, that is, being a person is a matter of stipulation, just as we might stipulate what counts as "out of bounds" in our pick-up game of football. If you reflect on this suggestion as applied to persons, however, it may not seem right. Imagine that country K takes over the world and decrees that heretofore all human beings with an IQ less than 100 are not persons. Country K might even enforce this rule with the result that those of less than average IQ come to be used for invasive experiments and as forced organ donors for the rest of society. Any dissenters to this policy, no matter their IQ, are liquidated. As a result, the new society stipulates that "person" shall be used only to refer to those with above-average IQ, and, of course, after some time everyone is using the word accordingly. In spite of the new stipulation, however, this does not seem to be a case in which a change has been made in what it is to *be* a person. For instance, some inhabitants of country K might (secretly) feel that their rulers have made an unjust decree. They might feel that their rulers are mistaken in treating these less intelligent human beings as nonpersons. We would not seem to be able to prove these skeptics wrong by claiming that being a person is a matter of convention or decree.

Again, in many societies it is only within the last few centuries that women have come to be viewed as persons rather than as property of their husbands. If you were to travel through time and visit one of the societies in which women were treated as property rather than persons, you would probably feel that the society is mistaken in treating women as nonpersons, in spite of that society's conventions. If you take that view, though, you are in effect denying that being a person is a matter of convention or decree. So how else might we make progress on what it is to be a person? A first step is to distinguish two different questions that may be asked with the words, "What is a person?"

Synchronic and Diachronic Questions of Identity

A question is *synchronic* if it concerns how things are at a certain time. We are thus asking a synchronic question when we ask how many skyscrapers in the world are currently over 1,000 feet in height. By contrast, we ask a *diachronic* question when we are concerned with how things are over a stretch of time. Asked in the year 2010, the question how many skyscrapers were built after the year 2000 is a diachronic question. The reason is that it can only be answered by looking over an interval of time rather than at a discrete moment.

Diachronic questions of identity concern what it is for a thing to persist over time. Our common sense tends to agree that a physical object can do so even if it undergoes some changes in its composition. You are constantly shedding and growing new skin cells, and red blood cells in your bloodstream are constantly dying and being replaced by new ones. Most of us would agree that these facts do not prevent you, as a person, from persisting through those changes. (We do sometimes hear remarks like, "Javier is a new man now that he's finally given up smoking." However, this is probably a bit of hyperbole. We don't think that after his last cigarette Javier died, and that the Javier before us has been resurrected. Rather, the phrase "new man" here is merely used to highlight how much more energetic and healthy looking Javier is now that he has kicked the habit.)

Our common-sense ways of thinking about how objects persist through time even permit the possibility of an object doing so while losing all of the matter of which it is composed. Suppose a beautiful, new, three-masted sailing ship named the *Harry Stottle* is launched from the port of New London in the year 1800. It goes on a long journey and returns safely to port in 1801. Before going to sea again, the *Harry Stottle* needs to have some of its rotting planks replaced. After the repairs are completed, off it goes and a year it later returns to port to have a few other bad planks removed. This process continues for an entire century, by the end of which a careful accountant, after reviewing notes taken of all repairs done over the last century, is surprised to find that not a single plank (or other bit of matter) on the *Harry Stottle* in the year 1900 was on it in the year 1800! It nevertheless seems to be the same ship, in spite of the entire change in material composition. Note that we would probably not say this if, in the year 1850, an extremely detailed and accurate blueprint of the *Harry Stottle* was made, the entire ship was burned to ashes, and now a ship is built precisely according to the blueprint. The resulting ship might be called the *Harry Stottle*, but if we know its history, we would probably agree that what we have before us is an excellent replica of the ship that burned down, and not the original *Harry Stottle* restored to its former glory.

If we agree that in the first case of piecemeal replacement of parts, the *Harry Stottle* has survived the entire nineteenth century, we are in effect agreeing that a thing can persist through changes in some of the parts of which it is composed. Most likely those changes cannot be too drastic in any brief time period. So long as they are gradual, however, diachronic identity would seem not to be ruled out. This point will be useful to bear in mind when we consider the arguments of the next chapter.

In contrast to the synchronic question, "What is a person?" we may also be asking the diachronic question what it is for a person to persist *through* time. This latter question is a bit more complicated than the synchronic question. To formulate it more fully, imagine that P_1 is a moment of a person's life. P_1 is evanescent while the person's life may be very long, yet P_1 will contain experiences, thoughts, emotions, and probably also memories. P_1 is what we may call a *person-stage*. Imagine now that P_2 is also a person-stage, and that it occurs later than P_1. In asking the diachronic question of personal identity, we are asking what it is for a later person-stage such as P_2 to belong to the same person as the earlier stage P_1. For instance, in the movie *The Return of Martin Guerre* (directed by Daniel Vigne), a man abandons his young wife and the medieval French village in which they live, and no one hears word of him for many years. After over a decade, an older man returns to both the village and the woman, professing to be the man who left years ago. The older man knows a great deal about the woman and the village, and many people take him for the man who left earlier. In asking the diachronic question of personal identity, we are asking what it is for this later stage to be one and the same person who left the village years ago.

With this clarification in aid of understanding personal identity we will be trying to fill in the ellipses in the following two different questions:

> *The synchronic question of personal identity*: Person-stage P_1 is a person if and only if . . .

> *The diachronic question of personal identity*: Person stage P_1 is a stage of the same person as person-stage P_2 if and only if . . .

We will approach the synchronic question first.

Synchronic Personal Identity

The case of *Homo floresiensis* might seem a bit esoteric. However, questions about what it takes to be person in the synchronic sense are hotly debated today, and in some cases entire social policies depend on how we answer them. For instance, proponents of the Great Ape Project have mounted a campaign to include other great apes—chimpanzees, gorillas, orangutans, bonobos—among the category of persons. On their website one can read a statement of their overarching mission:

> The Great Ape Project is an idea, a book, and an organization. The idea is radical but simple: to include the non-human great apes within the community of equals by granting them the basic moral and legal protection that only human beings currently enjoy. The book, which is the collective work of a group of scientists and scholars, is a multifaceted argument against the unthinking denial of fundamental rights to beings who are not members of our own species, but who quite evidently possess many of the characteristics that we consider morally important. The organization is an international group founded to work for the removal of the non-human great apes from the category of property, and for their immediate inclusion within the category of persons.
>
> (www.greatapeproject.org)

If we agree with the central contention of the Great Ape Project, we will accept great apes as persons. As we mentioned a moment ago, doing so will require the ascription of certain basic rights to great apes, and this change will almost certainly require modification of current practices. For instance, your great uncle might be rather strange, and he might do things that have to be seen to be believed. If, however, I were to suggest to you that we should put him in a zoo for all to see, you'd probably be offended, and you might reply with a remark such as, "I admit that Uncle Morris is odd, but he's a person, not an animal; you can't put him in a zoo!" That is quite a reasonable thing to say. However, if the contention of the Great Ape Project is correct, then we have no right displaying gorillas, orangutans, and other great apes in zoos either.

Similar points apply to torture, experimentation, and destruction of habitat for any of the great apes.

If the Great Ape Project is to convince the world of its claims, it will have to explain what morally important characteristics make an entity a person. Presumably the proponents of this movement will not argue that great apes have souls, since it is hard to know how they could convince the world of this claim. More plausibly, one might propose that a degree of self-consciousness is a sufficient, if perhaps not a necessary, condition for being a person. If that is plausible, then we may now note that *great apes do show evidence of a form of self-consciousness*. For example, a chimpanzee shows considerable evidence of understanding that what she sees in a mirror is herself there rather than another chimp. Given a hand mirror, for instance, she will promptly use it to examine two areas that she cannot normally see—the inside of her mouth and her private parts.[2]

We might well reflect on whether being a *Homo sapiens* is necessary and sufficient for being a person. Perhaps that biological category is arbitrary if our concern is with persons as moral agents. This, at least, is the contention of the Great Ape Project, and that contention is not one that we can rule out immediately unless we are to be dogmatic. More generally, self-consciousness seems a not unreasonable criterion for synchronic identity. However, as I just indicated, if we set this up as a necessary, rather than just sufficient, condition for being a person, we will have trouble counting infants as persons; likewise for those with severe mental disability. One challenge, then, as you consider the nature of synchronic identity, is to include as many members of our own species as possible who merit that treatment, without ruling out other species and possible beings arbitrarily. This question will only become more pressing in the years to come as we increase our understanding of species other than ourselves, and perhaps even discover intelligent life elsewhere in the universe. In the meantime we do well to turn to diachronic questions.

Memory Links and Identity over Time

A natural first thought about how we might answer the question raised by *The Return of Martin Guerre* is this: the man who returns many years later is the same person as the one who left earlier just in case the returning man can *remember* things that happened to the earlier stage. This point requires an immediate clarification. We occasionally seem to remember things that did not in fact happen to us. Perhaps you've had a vivid dream in which an owl eyed you warily as you passed under a tree in which it was perched. A few days later you find yourself unable to tell whether you really did see such an owl or instead just dreamed it. Cases of this kind I shall call *apparent memory* to distinguish them from *genuine memory*. All memories are ones in which we appear to recall something that happened to us in the past. Only some of these are genuine, and to be not just apparent but also genuine, the memory must be caused in the right way by the initial experience.[3] With this distinction between genuine and apparent memories in hand, we may now clarify our earlier hypothesis as follows:

> *Diachronic personal identity theory 1*: Person stage P_1 is a stage of the same person as person-stage P_2 if and only if P_2 can genuinely remember experiences had by P_1.

With apologies for the spoiler, the later person-stage calling himself "Martin Guerre" only *apparently* remembers experiences had by the earlier person-stage of Martin Guerre. The man who returns to the village is an imposter who had befriended the real Martin abroad and learned so much about him that he decided to attempt to stand in for him back in Martin's village. Unfortunately, the real Martin eventually shows up back in the village and unmasks the imposter, who is hanged for his impersonation. That series of events comports with our *diachronic theory 1* above, for the imposter who comes to the village only seems to remember experiences had by the earlier person-stage, but does not genuinely remember them. This theory also makes good sense of John Locke's famous case of the prince and the cobbler.[4] Modifying the case for present purposes, imagine a prince whose brain and other parts of his central nervous system have been transplanted one night into the body of a cobbler; a symmetrical operation has been performed on the cobbler. Here it seems very plausible that the prince wakes up with the body of a cobbler, and the cobbler with the body of the prince. One might explain that fact by noting that the later person-stage of the prince, waking up in the cobbler's bed, can remember experiences had by the earlier person-stage of the prince surrounded by courtesans. Likewise the later person-stage of the cobbler, waking up in the prince's bed, can remember experiences had by the earlier person-stage of the cobbler surrounded by the tools of his modest trade. It seems that both the prince and the cobbler have had "body transplants" while retaining their central nervous systems.

This diachronic theory of personal identity over time is due to Locke and is sometimes referred to as a form of *psychological continuity theory*. It is not without its detractors. For instance, the Scottish philosopher Thomas Reid (1710–96), writing a century after Locke, challenged Locke's very reliance on psychological continuity as the deciding factor. Reid first suggests that while psychological continuity might be *evidence* of personal identity over time, it is not what *makes* for such identity over time. Reid expands on the challenge as follows:

> Although memory gives the most irresistible evidence of my being the identical person that did such a thing, at such a time, I may have other good evidence of things which befell me, and which I do not remember: I know who bare me, and who suckled me, but I do not remember these events.
>
> (*Essays on the Intellectual Powers of Man*,
> Cambridge, MA: MIT Press)

Try as I may, I cannot remember being nursed by my mother at age six weeks, though she assures me that I did nurse at this age. Surely, though, I am the same person as the one who was nursed by her those many years ago? Further, even if you doubt that I was a person as an infant, the same point applies to any experiences, at a tender age or not, of which I have no memory for whatever reason.

Reid poses a good challenge to Locke's psychological continuity theory, but that theory has the resources to respond to it. The reason is that we may weaken the theory while retaining its spirit. Perhaps I cannot remember things that befell me when I was a very young child. However, I can remember things that befell earlier person-stages, who could remember things that befell earlier person-stages, who could remember things that befell . . . all the way back to experiences had by the young child. Thus whereas Locke's original diachronic personal identity theory 1 suggests a picture like this:

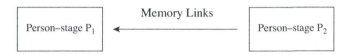

Figure 7.1 An Illustration of Diachronic Personal Identity Theory 1

A revised version of that theory would suggest a picture like the following:

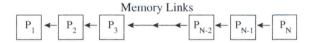

Figure 7.2 An Illustration of Diachronic Personal Identity Theory 2

where, as in Figure 7.1, all the arrows represent memory links. Here, so long as there are a finite number of person-stages between P_N and P_1, each of which can remember the preceding person-stage, then P_N and P_1 are stages of the same person. Further, you can slice things as finely as you like, so that two adjacent person-stages might be only a few moments apart from one another.

Brief reflection also shows that this modification is required to save Locke's theory from inconsistency even leaving aside Reid's objection. For imagine an old general (OG) who recalls his bravery on the battlefield as a young captain (YC). The young captain in turn remembers stealing apples from a neighbor's tree as a little boy (LB).[5] According to Locke's theory, OG is one and the same person as YC, and YC is one and the same person as LB. Further, identity generally, and personal identity specifically, seem to be transitive; that is, if A is the same person as B, and B is the same person as C, then A is the same person as C. Hence it follows on Locke's theory that OG is the same person as

LB. However, Locke's theory also denies that OG is the same person as LB, for OG neither does nor can remember experiences had by LB. Hence that theory requires a modification such as the following:

> *Diachronic personal identity theory 2:* Person-stage P_1 is a stage of the same person as person-stage P_N (where N is finite) if and only if P_N can genuinely remember experiences had by person-stage P_{N-1}, which can remember experiences had by person-stage P_{N-2}, which can remember . . . which can remember experiences had by person-stage P_1.

Figure 7.2 above illustrates this theory, which accounts for the old general case, as well as permitting Locke a cogent reply to Reid. However, we are not yet out of the woods. Two kind of cases pose problems even for the diachronic identity theory 2. These are cases involving amnesia as well as what is sometimes called person-fission. For the first kind of case, consider Lenny from the movie, *Memento* (directed by Christopher Nolan). Lenny has had an accident resulting in a severe form of amnesia known as anterograde amnesia. Although he can recall things from before the accident, he literally can't make new memories. In one chase scene in the movie, for instance, he cannot remember whether he is chasing the other guy or the other guy is chasing him! To make matters worse, in spite of having tattooed various alleged facts onto his skin, Lenny cannot be sure whether the person-stage that tattooed those statements had his facts straight. Now consider two person-stages of Lenny existing after the accident. Because of the severity of his amnesia, these two stages cannot be connected along the lines of diachronic identity theory 2. Yet it seems clear that they are two stages of the same person. Can you think of a way of changing the letter while retaining the spirit of diachronic personal identity theory 2, in order to deal with the puzzling case of Lenny?

Another problem for the Lockean theory is as follows. Suppose Morgan suffers from epilepsy, and doctors choose to sever her corpus calossum (the network of fibers connecting the left and right hemispheres of her brain) in order to minimize the danger of seizures. Now the two hemispheres of her brain have no way of communicating with each other. After some time, however, it emerges that many other systems in Morgan's body are failing. As a result the two hemispheres have to be removed and transplanted to a new body. But due to a clerical error at the hospital on the day of the operation, hemisphere L is put into one body while hemisphere R is put into another. (Neither host body had a working brain in it before, and both had been kept on life support by advanced machines.) After some recovery time, both L and R emerge from the hospital and try to resume a normal existence. Both L and R recall pre-operation life as Morgan. Neither L nor R is the same person as the other: they could, for instance, encounter each other at a bar, and vehemently disagree with each other on an important political question or football match! But the diachronic identity theory implies that they are stages of one person. After all, each is memory-linked to Morgan, and it would seem that if L is the same person as

Morgan, and Morgan is the same person as R, then L is the same person as R. Yet while dissociative identity disorder seems to be a case of multiple people simultaneously inhabiting a single body, it seems implausible that L and R could be stages of one and the same person.

Bodily Continuity and Identity over Time

Perhaps a defender of the psychological continuity theory will be able to think up a new diachronic identity theory in response to the problems we have just raised. Even if she can do so, however, it seems that there is something more fundamentally wrong about the theory. To see why, consider yet another case. Imagine a machine, the Duplicator/3-D Flesh Printer, which could make a molecule-for-molecule duplicate of you, including everything in your central nervous system, where, presumably, your memories are stored. If that duplicate of you were created, it would at least *appear* to remember things that happened earlier in your life: It can describe in detail your seventh birthday party, your high school graduation, what you had for lunch yesterday, and so forth. You are now faced with the opportunity of entering the duplicator machine. Oh, yes! There's one small issue I forgot to mention: after the duplication process is complete, the body that entered the machine will be destroyed in order to prevent confusion among your family, friends, employers, and so forth. The question is now: even if you are certain that the duplicator machine will make a perfectly accurate copy of your body, would you enter it?

I don't think I would. Perhaps I'm just being cowardly, but my sense is that if I were to enter that machine, a copy of me would be made, I would then be destroyed, and then some other being just like me would come into existence. (With luck he will take over my roles in life so that I won't be missed!) If you were considering entering that machine, wouldn't you, too, feel that among other things you were about to be killed? If you do feel this way, then that is reason for doubting any version of the psychological continuity theory.

Perhaps, then, Thomas Reid was right in suggesting that psychological continuity is, at best, evidence of personal identity over time but is not what constitutes it. Yet what other theory might we offer to explain personal identity over time? Perhaps the body is more important to diachronic identity than we have given it credit for thus far. Even in our Locke-inspired example of the prince and the cobbler, we did assume that each person gets to retain his central nervous system. Further, while various neurons in my central nervous system can be replaced one by one over a long period of time, and perhaps also large numbers of them can be replaced at once with a prosthetic device yet to be invented, it is hard to see how I could lose my *entire* central nervous system in one fell swoop and survive the change. This observation suggests another criterion of diachronic identity:

> *Diachronic personal identity theory 3:* Person-stage P_1 is a stage of the same person as person-stage P_2 if and only if P_1 and P_2 share the same body or same body component such as their central nervous system.

Given what we observed above about the *Harry Stottle* case, having the same body over time allows some change in parts. So you can satisfy this most recent definition if you lose and gain skin cells, or even have a finger amputated. This is as it should be, since we not inclined to suppose that I will cease to exist if I lose a skin cell or even a finger. Also, this theory makes good sense of many societies' practices in keeping track of personal identity over time. For instance, to determine whether the suspect in front of us is the person who committed a certain heinous crime a year ago, we will likely resort to fingerprints, and, if possible, DNA evidence to answer this question. Further, even if he cannot recall committing the crime, we might still rely upon physical evidence to show that he is the one who performed it. (His ability to recall the crime seems more relevant to how we punish him if he is found guilty.) That suggests that according at least to forensic science, bodily (as opposed to psychological) continuity is the heart of diachronic identity.

You might challenge diachronic personal identity theory 3 by remarking that many major religious traditions have a well-entrenched conception of disembodied survival after death. Disembodied survival does seem conceivable, even to many who are not theists. Further, if disembodied survival is possible, then bodily continuity is not required for diachronic identity. However, as we learned from Ryle's objection to Descartes in Chapter 3, not everything conceivable is really possible, and in particular we may have doubts about the possibility of an entirely non-physical mind. How could such a thing behave intelligently, or even be disposed to? The proponent of the bodily continuity theory might point out further that if survival after the destruction of the body were really possible, then it should also be possible for not just one, but *two* beings to exist, *both* of whom seem to recall vividly my life here on Earth. Each of these disembodied beings has as good a right to be counted as me as does the other. Which one is me? Are they both me? If so, then, by transitivity of identity, they are one person also, just inhabiting two different states of consciousness. This seems very strange. On the other hand, if one of them is me, but not the other, what, if anything, could make this the case? In fact, there could be thousands of disembodied beings all of whom are vying for the status of being me!

These consequences suggest why the proponent of the bodily continuity theory of diachronic identity might, as Ryle was, be skeptical that disembodied existence is really possible, and her skepticism would not be without basis. For that reason, we cannot refute the bodily continuity theory by invoking claims about life after death. Yet the bodily continuity theory seems hard to swallow even after the above clarifications. Not many people can resist the temptation to think that we could survive the destruction of our bodies, including our central nervous systems. It is the same sentiment that enabled Descartes to argue for his dualism in Chapter 3 on the basis of the possibility of surviving the death of one's body. In fact, it is the same sentiment that enabled Socrates to drink hemlock with equanimity after being sentenced to death by his fellow Athenians for allegedly corrupting the youth of the city. If diachronic identity consists in bodily continuity, however, these sentiments are illusory. Could that really be?

If so, then philosophy teaches us that some of our most heartfelt convictions need to be let go.

In this chapter we have explored a few of the more prominent accounts of personhood (both synchronic and diachronic) in the Western philosophical tradition. We have only skated along the surface of this topic, but I hope to have given you a feel for some of the central issues. Our next task will be to examine a radically opposed tradition of thought according to which the posit of a self is a form of convenient mythology that we do better to give up. This tradition would call for a dramatically revised understanding of what it is to know ourselves.

Chapter Summary

- Synchronic personal identity concerns what it is for an object (such as a hunk of flesh or a machine) to be a person at a time, whereas diachronic personal identity concerns what it is for one temporally located "person-stage" to be a stage of one and the same person as a "person stage" at a different time.
- Synchronic personal identity questions cannot be answered by stipulating that human beings are identical to persons. "Human being" refers to a biological category, whereas it is controversial to assume that "person" must do so. Synchronic questions are made pressing by, for instance, discovery of new species different from our own but who display considerable intelligence.
- A psychological continuity theory of diachronic personal identity appeals to memory links between one person stage and others prior to it. Such a theory needs refinement in light of counterexamples involving "person fission" and memory loss.
- Appreciating the bodily continuity theory of diachronic identity is aided by considering examples in which a material object persists over time while losing and have many (or even all) of its parts replaced over that period.
- For both the psychological and bodily continuity theories, a person's persistence over time does not require that there is a single component (such as a psychological state or group of neural tissues) that persists throughout their existence.

Study Questions

1. Please explain the difference between diachronic and synchronic questions of personal identity. What is John Locke's original, unrefined view of diachronic personal identity? In light of this position, explain why Locke holds that a person can survive the loss of her body, and even the loss of her brain? Next, show how Locke attempts to bolster his thesis by means of his example of the prince and the cobbler.

2. Is Locke's theory of diachronic personal identity compatible with the possibility of more than one person inhabiting a single body, as appears to be the case with clinical examples of multiple personality? Please explain your answer.

3. Thomas Reid denies that diachronic personal identity requires continuity of memory. After explaining the Old General Paradox, show how it is a challenge to Locke's unrefined theory of diachronic personal identity. Could Locke refine this theory of diachronic personal identity in order to accommodate the Old General Paradox? Please explain your answer.

4. How might the example of *Memento's* Lenny, who suffers from antero-grade amnesia, challenge even Locke's refined theory of diachronic personal identity?

5. Why might it be thought that any theory of diachronic personal identity founders on the possibility "fission," in which one person's memories seem to be transferred into two different bodies?

6. Assuming that you have no desire to commit suicide, would you step into a "duplicator machine" as described in this chapter? Please explain your answer.

7. How might one defend a conception of diachronic personal identity in terms of bodily continuity?

8. Does the bodily continuity theory leave open the possibility of surviving the total destruction of your body?

9. Suppose a defender of the Great Ape Project tries to argue that, for instance, chimpanzees should be counted as persons just as much as human beings should. How might she defend that conclusion? Might empirical research be relevant to supporting or rebutting her contention? Please explain your answer.

10. Please explain what it might mean to modify one's own will. Might the ability to modify one's own will be pertinent to the issue of being a person in the synchronic sense? Please explain your answer. Might the ability to modify one's own will be pertinent to the issue of having free will? Please explain your answer.

Notes

1. "Eton or the Zoo," from the *BBC World Service,* Friday, October 29, 2004. A rigorous discussion of the anthropological issues may be found in D. Argue, D. Donlon, C. Groves, and R. Wright (2006) "*Homo floresiensis*: Microcephalic, Pygmoid, Aus-tralopithecus, or Homo?" *Journal of Human Evolution*, vol. 51, pp. 360–74.

2. For evidence supporting such claims, some of the essays in K. Andrews and J. Beck (eds.) (2017) *Routledge Companion to the Philosophy of Animal Minds* (New York and London: Routledge) will be helpful.

3. This notion of "being caused in the right way" is difficult to pin down, but in what follows I will assume that it is possible to elucidate it in a non-circular way.

4. J. Locke (1975) *Essay Concerning Human Understanding*, ed. P. Nidditch (Oxford: Oxford University Press), p. 30.

5. This example is drawn from J. Perry (2008) "Introduction," in J. Perry (ed.) *Personal Identity* (Berkeley: University of California Press), p. 17.

Introductory Further Reading

Kind, A. (2015) *Persons and Personal Identity* (Malden, MA: Polity Press). Accessible, up-to-date introduction to central philosophical problems of personal identity.

Locke, J. (1975) *Essay Concerning Human Understanding*, ed. P. Nidditch (Oxford: Oxford University Press). A major text of Western philosophy, including a famous presentation of Locke's theory of psychological continuity.

Perry, J. (1978) *A Dialogue on Personal Identity and Immortality* (Indianapolis: Hackett). Highly readable fictional dialogue touching on central problems of personal identity.

Advanced Further Reading

Gunnarsson, L. (2010) *The Philosophy of Personal Identity and Multiple Personality* (New York: Routledge). Psychologically informed account of personal identity with special attention to multiple-personality disorder.

Perry, J. (1978) *Personal Identity* (Berkeley: University of California Press). A collection of classic articles (historical and contemporary) on core problems of personal identity.

———. (2002) *Identity, Personal Identity, and the Self* (Indianapolis: Hackett).

Schechtman, M. (1996) *The Constitution of Selves* (Ithaca, NY: Cornell University Press). Influential defense of a "narrative" view of personal identity.

8 No Thyself
A Buddhist Perspective

Introduction

In stark opposition to the Western approach to the self is the Buddhist. We introduce Buddhism by explaining how it is not a religion in the traditional sense, and highlight those strands of Buddhism that see it as a physically and intellectually rigorous way of answering philosophical questions. Integral to much Buddhist tradition is also an urgency to alleviate suffering (both in oneself and in others), which is thought to stand in the way of enlightenment. Some Buddhist traditions hold that one source of suffering is fixation on a view of oneself *as* a self, and our main aim in this chapter is to understand the Buddhist considerations against the view that there is any diachronic or even synchronic personal identity. We consider two famous Buddhist arguments to this effect, one stemming from a documented conversation between a monk Nāgasena and one King Milinda. Nāgasena's arguments are not conclusive against the idea of a synchronic self, but it is still illuminating to imagine what it would be like to let go of the idea of that we are persons. We explore the implications of such a renunciation, suggesting that one's life might go better once one eschews commitment to a view of oneself *as* a self.

Buddhism as a Non-Religion

We have discovered in the previous pages that through either introspection or extrospection, we can learn new things about ourselves, including things that are surprising or even disturbing. However, we have also found that sometimes, when we try to peer within, there is less to see than we had hoped. In particular, if we try to introspect in search of our "true selves," we are likely to be disappointed. Questions such as "What do I *really* want?" or "What am I *really* like?" have a table-thumping demandingness that likely will not be satisfied even by intensive self-scrutiny. Rather, if we are to make progress on questions such as these, a more responsible approach will be to recognize that their answers are as much *made* as *found*: to a considerable extent we have to decide what we want, and what we are like. Further, while we do not have complete leeway in such matters (at least at this point in my life, there are many high-level skills that are unattainable for me even if I wish I could acquire them), given an early enough start, and sufficient time and tenacity, we have plenty of scope for making ourselves. Perhaps the above two questions are better replaced with "What *shall* I want?" and "Who *shall* I be?"

An ancient source of doubt about the idea that we harbor a self there to be discovered is the Buddhist tradition. Although the term "Buddhist" covers a vast and overlapping network of traditions and practices, our emphasis here will be on those aspects of Buddhism stressing a number of themes. One of these themes distinguishes Buddhism from what are properly called religions. Religions properly so-called include taking certain doctrines, such as the existence of a divine being or that of an afterlife, on faith: adherents to, say, Christianity, Islam, and Judaism are expected to believe in a divine being even if there is not compelling evidence in favor of that proposition. In this respect religion demands an epistemic double-standard: one has a lower threshold for what is allowed in believing in a divine being than is required, for, say, coming to a conclusion about what drove the dinosaurs to extinction or the cause of Crohn's disease.

Another distinguishing feature of paradigm cases of religions is their positing of a divine being that is held to be worthy of worship. While some religious traditions take their god to be capable of vengeance and to possess other attributes that may in the view of some be moral failings, for the most part the major religions of the world posit divine beings with properties such as omnipresence (knowing everything that there is to know), omnipotence (being able to do everything that it is possible to do), and omnibenevolence (having all virtues that it is possible to have) that make them worthy of human worship. Finally, the great religions of the world tend to adhere to a doctrine of salvation: their adherents are told that depending either on fate or their actions during their lives, they may have a chance of an afterlife that will be desirable in some way. Perhaps they will experience union with the aforementioned divine being, or a kind of bliss that goes on eternally.

Buddhism as discussed here eschews all three of the above aspects of religion as typically understood. First of all, it does not ask us to take anything on faith, but instead merely asks us to use our reasoning faculties to the best of our abilities to discern our nature and facts about the world around us. Second, Buddhism does not posit any divine beings, or at least divine beings worthy of worship. Buddha himself is revered by many Buddhists, but is respected as being someone very wise and accomplished, just as we might respect the winner of the Nobel Peace Prize or a great novelist. Finally, Buddhists do not promise their adherents any salvation in an afterlife of bliss, union with a divine being, and so forth. For Buddhists there is such a thing as enlightenment, but this can be achieved during your lifetime and does not require the cooperation of anyone else, divine or otherwise. Instead, enlightenment is merely the understanding of our nature and of our place in the world.

Overcoming Suffering

The historical person who came to be known as Buddha was originally named Gautama. Scholarly opinions differ as to his exact dates, but the consensus is that he lived in the fifth century BC. He was born into comfortable circumstances in the city-state of Kapilavatsu in what is now the western part of Nepal. Gautama was dissatisfied with the prevailing Vedic religion of his day and chose to become a śramaṇa, or wandering renunciant who devotes his life to answering spiritual questions. Gautama shared with many other śramaṇas the conviction that we can only find happiness by overcoming our ignorance of our true nature. Doing so involves not only intellectual inquiry, but also bodily rigors such as fasting, sitting motionless for long periods of time, refraining from sleep, yogic techniques, and meditative practices such as concentrating on a single object for as long as possible.

After seeking guidance from other śramaṇas and being dissatisfied with the results, Gautama struck out on his own. One evening he happened upon an isolated grove in a forest and resolved to spend the rest of the night in contemplation. Over the next several hours and with the aid of a series of yogic techniques, Gautama felt himself to have achieved enlightenment: he had solved what was thought to be a basic problem of human existence, and resolved to impart the knowledge thus obtained to others. In so doing he became what is known as a Buddha.

The basic problem in question was the nature of human suffering and how it might be overcome. According to the Buddha's way of thinking, suffering comes in three forms, listed in increasing order of subtlety. The first such form of suffering is simply the varieties of what we might think of as first-order pain: a cut finger, a broken arm, diseased lungs, and the like are all sources of pain and thereby of suffering. Connected with these is often a second-order pain, or at least distress: if I am aware of something amiss with my health, that will likely cause me anxiety about whether I can do all the things I would like to do, either because my life will be cut short, or because my range of activities will be limited. Either way, the physical pain often brings with it a further dimension of psychic pain. The first form of suffering, then, is due to physical pain and the psychic distress that might accompany it.

The second form of suffering concerns impermanence. According to Buddha and those who came to follow his teachings, we also experience suffering even in procuring the things that we desire. Imagine you buy a new pair of shoes. These garner some compliments and do a bit to improve your confidence. However, with every step you take, they wear down ever so slightly, and are that much closer to being discarded. Further, each new day brings the possibility of this style's going out of fashion. According to Buddha it is considerations like these that show that even those things that give fleeting pleasure also bring with them a dimension of suffering. This is known as suffering due to impermanence.

The third form of suffering is the least straightforward and the most controversial. According to the Vedic tradition in which Buddha was brought up, subsequent to the destruction of our bodies at death, we will be reborn, possibly as another kind of creature such as a sparrow or a salmon. It might seem at first glance that such a rebirth could be very interesting: after all, it would be lovely to fly in my sparrow body without—as I did back in my human days—having to be stuck in an airplane or risk my life base-jumping! On the other hand, one might feel that this karmic cycle of deaths and rebirths raises the question: what is the point of the entire process? Granted, on the karmic doctrine I get to live a series of lives rather than just one. But if it is unclear what the point of this current life is, how could that question be resolved by my participating in a long series of such lives?

It might be replied here that just because most of the things we do have a point (I cut vegetables in order to cook them, cook them in order to eat them, eat the resulting dish for pleasure as well as to stay energetic and healthy, etc.) it does not follow that my entire life must have a point. Nor does my entire life need to have a point in order for the activities that make it up to do so. Many of those activities can be worthwhile for their own sake rather than for the sake of something else. (There need not be a *point* in loving someone, for instance; one just does.) The Buddhist tradition will counter that while it is true that one can enjoy a certain measure of happiness while on the karmic treadmill of death and rebirth, that happiness will always be limited by our failing to recognize that the idea of a self as persisting through these changes, or even through a single biological life, is illusory. This brings us to the Buddhist doctrine of "non-self."

Arguments against a Persisting Self

One central facet of Buddhist views of how best to avoid suffering is the suggestion that we should forego our belief in selves, or persons. That suggestion poses a challenge to the entire project of understanding self-knowledge: if there's no self, then there is apparently no self to know. This is why when I teach courses on self-knowledge, when we encounter this Buddhist doctrine I like to point out that the course has changed its name to "No Thyself." But the idea that there is no self probably at first glance seems bizarre—perhaps even self-contradictory. Nonetheless our task in this section will be to understand why some important strands of Buddhist thought reject persons, as well as to discern how we might give up this preconception. Could it even make sense to give up on the idea that you are a person?

We emphasized in Chapter 7 the importance of distinguishing between diachronic and synchronic questions of identity: diachronic questions of identity concern the persistence of an object over time, and pose such questions as what it is for this piece of wax at time t_1 to be the same entity as that piece of wax at time t_2. By contrast, synchronic questions concern what it is for an entity to have a certain characteristic, such as being alive, or being a mammal, or being a person, at a particular time. An answer to a diachronic question may not provide an answer to the synchronic, nor vice versa. In this section we will for the most part bracket synchronic questions of personal identity and focus on diachronic questions.

Why might someone deny that persons persist through time? We noted in the last chapter that Thomas Reid criticized John Locke by saying that while "memory links" provide very good evidence that I am one and the same person as the one who existed some years ago, they are not what makes me the same person. Reid for this reason rejected Locke's theory as an account of what makes personal identity over time, but he did not have another theory to put in its place. Instead, he held that the notion of diachronic personal identity is a primitive notion that cannot be explained in any more fundamental terms. But that is not at all the same as rejecting the reality of personal identity, which Reid took to be a genuine and important phenomenon.

To get a better feel for where the Buddhist doctrine of "non-self" is coming from, observe that it is not easy to identify what aspect of ourselves does persist over time if in fact we do persist. Experiences are evanescent, emotions are ephemeral, and beliefs are subject to change as new facts come in or as memory fades. If we do persist through time, it is not entirely clear what aspect of ourselves accounts for this fact. What's more, it is easy to get the impression that something is persisting through time even in situations in which, were we to examine the facts more carefully, we would realize that nothing is. For instance, imagine an array of neon lights organized into the shape of a rectangle. Each one might turn on and off in a way synchronized with the other lights so that there *appears* to be a light moving around the perimeter of the rectangle. However, once we inspect the array, we will likely give up the presupposition that there is a single light moving. Instead, there are just stationary lights turning on and off in such a way as to create this impression. Well, given that we are prone to fall for such illusions, we might wonder whether belief in a persisting self over time might be yet another.

One famous document from the Buddhist written tradition suggests a line of thought somewhat to this effect. To understand the line of thought, observe that the Sanskrit word "'skhanda" refers to any collection of things, and *rūpa* refers to that skhanda that contains all of your bodily things such as blood, skin, ligaments, hair, and internal organs. Here the Buddha is addressing some of his companions:

"What do you think, O monks? Is rūpa permanent, or transitory?"

"It is transitory, Reverend Sir."

"And that which is transitory, is it painful, or is it pleasant?"

"It is painful, Reverend Sir."

"And that which is transitory, painful, and liable to change, is it possible to say of it, 'This is mine; this am I; this is my self'?"

"Certainly not, Reverend Sir."

"Is feeling . . . perception . . . volition . . . consciousness, permanent or transitory?"

"It is transitory, Reverend Sir."

(S III.66–68; translation in Siderits' 2007)

Later in this passage, the Buddha argues that as with rūpa, so too with the other four skhandas: none of them can plausibly be identified with the self. M. Siderits reconstructs the Buddha's line of reasoning in the following way.

1. Rūpa is impermanent.
2. Sensation is impermanent.
3. Perception is impermanent.
4. Volition is impermanent.
5. Consciousness is impermanent.
6. There is no more to the self than these five skhandas.
7. If there were a self, it would be permanent.

Ergo,

8. There is no self.

(Siderits 2007, p. 39)

In saying, for instance, that sensation is impermanent, the contrast is not with an alleged sensation that would last forever. Rather, the idea is that there is no one sensation that seems to last as long as you do—or at least as long as you would if common sense is to be believed. Common sense holds that in general, when a human body lasts, say, 75 years, then there is a person who either is or inhabits that body and who survives for at least as long as the body does.[1] In this light, the most intuitive way to understand a premise such as (2) is as saying that no one sensation lasts for those entire 75 years.

Siderits presents the above argument as being valid, that is as having the feature that if all the premises are true, then the conclusion will be true as well. Even if that is so, we might still ask whether, for instance, rūpa is indeed impermanent. You may know, for instance, that the urban legend that all the cells in your body are replaced every seven years, is not quite true. Instead, apparently many of your brain cells last throughout your lifetime, and the cells in the lens of each of your eyes are also formed at birth and never replaced.[2] In this sense, premise 1 of the above argument is not, strictly, true. However, even if all the cells in our bodies were replaced in the course of our lifetimes—so that we are like the ship *Harry Stottle* discussed in Chapter 7—the above argument would still not show that the self does not persist through time.

The reason is that there is another way of understanding the idea that rūpa might be permanent. For recall from Chapter 7 that so-called bodily continuity may also be understood in more abstract terms, not as requiring a single item of matter following you throughout your life, but rather as requiring that all or most such items be integrally connected with one another. Most of us would agree that the ship, *Harry Stottle*, persists through time even if the vessel that returns to port in the year 1900 has not a single item of matter in common with the one that left port a century earlier. Given this, a defender of the bodily continuity theory of diachronic personal identity may also challenge premise (1) of the above argument by noting that even if no particular bit of rūpa survives as long as I do, that does not show that my body does not survive as long as I do. Instead, in the case of the ship, what are preserved over time are the higher-order properties of *having the same overall shape and function*, and of *being made of largely the same material as it was moments earlier*. These two properties, I contend, persist through the entire existence of the ship. Admittedly they are somewhat vague, but that is as it should be: after all, there are plenty of changes the *Harry Stottle* might undergo that would make us uncertain whether the thing that results is the same thing as before.

This is to say that even if the above argument is valid, we are justified in denying that it is sound, since we are justified in being skeptical of premise 1. The reason is that even if, contrary to fact, all my cells were replaced over my lifetime, I could still survive that change according to the bodily continuity theory: so long as the configuration and composition of my cells do not change radically over a short period, I can survive through those changes. Here too the vague characterization I have given in terms of "configuration and composition" is to be expected. It will predict that there will be cases in which we are simply not sure whether I have survived a bodily change. That is as we should expect.

One might also find reason for challenging premise 5. A defender of the psychological continuity theory of personal identity might point out that even if there is no one conscious experience that follows me throughout my entire existence, there might still be a higher-order feature that persists, namely the property of being *memory linked to earlier person-stages*. Aside from cases of complete amnesia, it would seem that a person-stage either does or can recall an experience had by an earlier person-stage, who can in return recall an experience had by . . . along the lines of the Diachronic Personal Identity Theory 2 of the previous chapter. The Lockean theory of identity based on psychological continuity, that is, can grant that our memories ebb and flow, while still holding that premise (5) is dubious: all the person-stages that make up me have the property of being memory-linked to earlier stages.

We do not have to choose sides between the bodily and psychological continuity theories. Instead, the point to stress is that either theory has a robust response to the Buddhist argument against a persisting self. That is not to say that the conclusion of that argument is untrue. Absence of proof is not proof of absence. But we are still in search of a reason to accept that conclusion.

You may at this point object that we have been anachronistic in our response to the Buddhist argument against a persisting self. After all, higher-order concepts such as being memory-linked to an earlier person-stage, are sophisticated recent innovations that cannot have been expected to occur to people two millennia ago, even Buddha and his followers. This may well be correct, and we should concede that for its time, the Buddhist argument against a persisting self may well have seemed persuasive even to critical and reflective listeners. However, our question is not whether the argument should have been convincing when it was first formulated, but rather whether we should also find it compelling now. I have argued that we should not do so. Of course, it is well within the rights of a contemporary defender of the Buddhist position, armed with current analytical techniques, to improve on the argument and win us over.

Arguments against a Synchronic Self

The Buddhist tradition also contains lines of thought purporting to show that there is also no personal identity in the synchronic sense. In a famous dialogue between one King Milinda and a Buddhist priest named Nāgasena, the latter argues that the king's name does not refer to a genuine person but is only a "convenient designator," that is, a term we use for convenience rather than because it refers to anything objectively real. Near the inception of their conversation, Nāgasena asks Milinda how he traveled to their meeting that day:

> "Sir, I did not go on foot. I came in a chariot."
>
> "Your majesty, if you came in a chariot, tell me what the chariot is. Pray, your, majesty, is the pole the chariot?"
>
> "Indeed not, sir."
>
> "Are the wheels the chariot?"
>
> "Indeed not, sir."
>
> . . .
>
> "Pray, your majesty, are pole, axle, wheels, chariot-body, banner-staff, yoke, reins, and goad unitedly the chariot?"
>
> "Indeed not, sir."
>
> "Your majesty, although I question you very closely, I fail to discover any chariot. Verily now, your majesty, the word chariot is a mere empty sound."
> (Siderits 2007, p. 53)

It is clear that the pole is not the chariot and that the wheels are not the chariot. But why might King Milinda deny that pole, axle, and so forth are "unitedly" the chariot? Siderits attempts to makes sense of this denial by reflecting on the nature of reduction. In particular he refers to what he terms the doctrine of *mereological reductionism*: if a composite object is composed of and can be reduced to its parts, then although the parts are real, the composite object is not real. It is, Siderits tells us, "not anything over and above the parts" (2007, p. 54).

Mereological reductionism as Siderits construes it is, however, a controversial view. To see why, contrast two cases. Imagine someone finds a narwhal tusk on a Scandinavian beach and declares, "I've found a unicorn horn!" We would be within our rights to reply, "No, what you found is a narwhal tusk. "Unicorn horns" are really just narwhal tusks." This remark is naturally understood as suggesting that there no such things as unicorn horns. By contrast when we learn that lightning is just electrical discharge (and not, say, emanations from an enraged Zeus), we are not inclined to infer that there are no such things as lightning bolts. Instead, we are more likely to continue to believe in lightning bolts, while at the same time being confident that we can explain what they consist in.

What is the difference between unicorn horns and lightning bolts, and why should we treat these two cases differently? The difference, I submit, is that we have independent reasons for disbelieving in unicorn horns, but no such reasons for disbelieving in lightning bolts. This is because believing in unicorn horns would seem to commit us to believing in unicorns, which are after all supernatural. This in turn would go against our best-supported, naturalistic view of how the world works. By contrast, while Ancient Greeks might have tied the concept of a lightning bolt to the activity of an enraged deity, modern viewers of the heavens do not do so. As a result, at least nowadays, speaking of lightning bolts does not commit a speaker to anything supernatural. For these reasons, we may distinguish between *eliminative reductions*, and *preservative reductions*. The former reduction is best taken to show that the thing being reduced does not exist, while the latter does not. This is why we may say, "Of course lightning is a real thing, and if you want an account of its nature, I can explain that as well."

Now which side do chariots occupy? Is the reduction of chariots to their components eliminative or preservative? That depends on whether believing in chariots commits us to something untoward. I suggest that it does not do so. Belief in chariots does not imply anything supernatural or otherwise at odds with our best scientific theories. Accordingly, while Nāgasena's discussion with King Milinda is a fascinating one, we should not be misled by it into thinking that chariots do not exist.

All this of course is prelude to the question whether persons, assuming that they can be reduced to the five skhandas, should be given an eliminative or a preservative reduction. This too depends on whether believing in persons commits us to something supernatural or otherwise untoward. While it is difficult to *define* what a person is in the synchronic sense, this does not show that belief in persons commits us to anything objectionable. Likewise, as we reflect on persons in the diachronic sense, we might be tempted to grapple with the puzzles that arise from the apparent possibility of persons surviving after death. However, our discussion of materialist approaches to personhood in the last chapter have shown us that a person might persist through time but cease to exist when her body is destroyed. If that view is correct, then it will prevent us from having to figure out what might happen if two person-stages in Heaven seem to remember experiences had by one and the same person-stage back on earth. Such mysteries do not have to arise just because we countenance a self persisting through time.

Losing Oneself

Even if we are not won over by the Buddhist arguments against persons in either the diachronic or synchronic senses, this does not mean that the conclusions of these arguments are incorrect. Again, absence of proof is not proof of absence. But does it even make sense to suppose that there are no selves, that is, that we are not persons? Did not Descartes' *cogito* argument show that from the mere fact that I am thinking, I can infer that I also exist? Yes, but this does not imply that the "I" used in Descartes' argument guarantees that it refers to a full-fledged person. What if, instead of persons, we think of ourselves as collections of the skhandas that the Buddhist argument above mentions: rūpa, consciousness, volitions, etc? We are, on this way of thinking, swarms or flocks of these things that as a result of the forces of evolution happen to hang together, but that do not need to be unified in any deeper way as would be done with the concept of a person. We don't feel compelled to unify the skhandas that make up a turtle or beaver by dignifying one of them with the term "person." Why should we need to do any differently in the case of our own species?

To this last question you might well reply that the difference between turtles and beavers on the one hand, and human beings on the other, is that we are superior to these other animals, and that superiority is captured by the idea that we are persons and they are not. To which the Buddhist philosopher might reply: perhaps it is true that we are more *intelligent* than other species (though we still have a lot to learn about animal intelligence, and may well be surprised as we find out more), and therefore are intellectually superior. However, why is this particular dimension of superiority one that pushes us over a special threshold while other dimensions do not? Dolphins can swim faster than we can; wolves have a better sense of smell than we do, and so on. Perhaps it is a form of narcissism to think that intelligence is more important than these other abilities in such a way as to be the only thing that qualifies a species for the "personhood" club?

A philosopher like Nāgasena will say, then, that we should try out the idea that we are not persons and see what happens. Perhaps we will find the experiment intriguing, and indeed even liberating. What is more, it may improve matters in and around the swarm that is you. Consider for instance the concepts of *greed* and *envy*. One who is greedy wants more of a particular good for himself than he truly needs. Similarly, one who is envious wants something that another person has but that he does not deserve. Neither greed nor envy seems like a particularly admirable trait. Instead, I might feel that things would go better in and around my swarm if I could get rid of both of these emotions. Giving up on the idea that I am a person might help me do so. Of course, it could also happen that my bodily desire for more food makes me eat greedily, and even envy the food that I see on your plate, even if we do not think of ourselves as persons distinct from other persons. On the other hand, sometimes when we lust for something that is not ours, we think, "I want that; I want that to be mine and not anyone else's!" This sentiment flows naturally from thinking of ourselves as persons distinct from other persons, and would be harder (though not impossible) to muster if we did not think of ourselves in this way.

A Buddhist philosopher will suggest a more general point that goes beyond greed and envy. The suggestion is that giving up on the idea of persons will help us behave more ethically. For one, once I jettison that idea I may be more willing to acknowledge instances of suffering associated with other swarms than the one right around here, and you could do the same for the swarms in your vicinity. In love, whether it be romantic love or the love of a mother for her child, the wants, needs, and hopes of one swarm tend to overlap with those of another swarm: we do what we do because it is helpful, not because one or the other of us specifically will be helped. So too in friendship, one friend might do something with little interest in the question whether she or her friend will benefit more than the other. More broadly, physical pain, as well as suffering more bound up with emotion such as loneliness, fear, regret, and shame, all seem to call out for us to alleviate them if we are able to, and to do so regardless of where we take the voice to be calling from. By contrast, while it is quite possible for someone who takes herself to be a person in the traditional Western sense in order to act compassionately, she must always cross a boundary to do so: she must on some level construe the situation as one self helping a distinct self. If, instead, we eschew the idea of ourselves as distinct persons, there will not be any boundary needing to be crossed.

In our exploration of self-knowledge we have considered classical Indian and Greek traditions of thought on the topic, as well as modern explorations of the issue either inspired or responding to a tradition begun by Descartes. We have not confined ourselves to discussions within philosophy proper, but have also looked at those considered part of psychoanalysis, social psychology, and to a lesser extent neuroscience. Instead of aiming for a comprehensive view of the topic, we have focused on highlights—or promontories to keep with the peripatetic metaphor with which this book began. Here are some of the more significant ones.

In the Western tradition since the time of Descartes, the self has been held to comprise character traits, as well as mental characteristics including cognitive, affective, and experiential states. In line with a distinction between propositional and ability knowledge, we may see that knowledge of this self consists in appreciation of its features as well as competence to manage its needs, concerns, aspirations, fears, and so forth. These two forms of knowledge complement each other. The value of self-knowledge thus construed consists not in the fact that knowledge is itself of intrinsic value. (Knowledge may be of intrinsic value, but that is not what explains the full value of self-knowledge.) Rather, self-knowledge has value due primarily to its connection to wisdom: one who knows how things are with her, and how to manage herself, is also more apt to make good choices both for herself and in relation to others. Other-directed wisdom is closely bound up with empathy, as well as with our ability to appreciate our psychological immune system while keeping a balance between our need to "spin" events and the importance of facing hard truths about ourselves. Introspection as commonly understood plays at best a supporting role in this enterprise; once, however, introspection is reinterpreted so as to include sensitivity to the "somatic markedness" of much experience, it is a useful guide particularly to one's affective situation. On this wisdom-centered approach to self-knowledge, there is little reason to think we would gain from achieving comprehensive self-knowledge even if such a thing were possible: for the most part, automatic processes can take care of themselves, and we become only minimally wiser by learning about them. Exceptions arise for dysfunctional aspects of such processes such as phobias, as well as for implicit biases.

The Indian Buddhist tradition challenges our very assumption of a self. Acknowledging that "self" and "person" facilitate convenient ways of speaking and thinking, this form of Buddhism advocates jettisoning the assumption of a self as a feature of objective reality and replacing it with a picture of a swarm or cloud of bodily features, behaviors, thoughts, emotions, experiences, and the like. We have seen that the arguments for this position are not conclusive. However, the conclusions of these arguments may nevertheless be correct, and we have suggested the "try it on for size" approach: stop thinking of yourself and others as persons, and focus instead on the swarms. Do things go better, both in and around this swarm and in relation to other swarms? If so, that is some reason for thinking it preferable to let go of thyself than to get too hung up on knowing it.

Is the examined life the only one worth living? This seems doubtful, given all the cases we have discussed in these pages of people who do good or even great things but who spend little time on self-examination either in the Socratic sense (of engaging in dialectic about life's most challenging issues), or in the more modern sense (involving a combination of introspection and extrospection). However, I hope to have made a case that self-examination, in either the Socratic or modern senses, improves one's prospects of making wise choices. One form of self-examination might lead you to admit to yourself that you bear a grudge toward someone, and such a realization might encourage you to discern the source of that feeling as well as a means of resolving it. Another form of self-examination might lead you to debate with others about whether a proposed government policy is just or is instead discriminatory toward a minority group in the country in which you live. That discussion might help you refine and sharpen your thinking about the proper role of government, and thereby lead you toward a more enlightened path as a voter and mentor to others. Yet a third form of self-examination, the fly-on-the-wall variety, might help you to conceive of some large-scale features of your life from a third-personal, self-distanced, point of view: "He began spending more time on his own," or, "She started to take up some hobbies that put her in the company of others more regularly." These perspectives on yourself can help you to consider whether the large-scale trajectory your life is on is the one you want it to be on, or instead whether it might be worth re-orienting yourself in some way. Accordingly, although the self-knowledge and the self-examination that aims toward it come in a daunting variety of shapes and sizes, we do well to take up the challenges they present. Let us just bear in mind that too much self-examination may become counter-productive: given the choice between yet another hour of self-examination, and going outside on a rainy day to splash around in puddles, I trust you'll know what to do.

Chapter Summary

- Unlike Islam, Judaism, or Christianity, Buddhism is not best thought of as religion: it does not posit a divine being, and does not promise an afterlife of eternal bliss so long as one believes or behaves in a certain way.
- Buddhism is instead best seen as a way of using our reasoning capacities to understand our true natures and to overcome suffering.
- Many strands within Buddhism have advocated a doctrine of non-self, according to which terms like "person" and "self" are merely convenient labels that do not pick out anything objectively real.
- Arguments for the "no-self" conclusion are intriguing, but in light of the psychological and bodily continuity theories discussed in Chapter 7, we may see how these arguments may be resisted.
- It may nevertheless be true that "self" is only a convenient designator. Our lives (including our social relationships) might go better by eschewing the posit of the self.
- In retrospect, we find that self-examination (whether in the form of Socratic dialectic, introspection, or extrospection) is conducive to living wisely and thus well. This does not guarantee that self-examination is always the best use of one's time and effort.

Study Questions

1. Why is it problematic to think of Buddhism as a religion?
2. What are the three kinds of suffering that the Buddhist philosophers recognize? How is the third kind related to the phenomenon of karmic rebirth?
3. Please reconstruct one Buddhist argument for a no-self conclusion (either of the synchronic or diachronic variety). Why might it be thought that this argument is not compelling?
4. What might it be like to give up the posit of yourself *as* a self? Does it make sense? Might it make your life go better? Please explain your answer.
5. How would you characterize the value and limits of self-knowledge? To the extent that you disagree with this book's author in your answer, please try to explain the source of that disagreement.

Notes

1. Some might hold that an infant falls into the biological category of a human being, but is not, or at least not yet, a person. So too, one who suffers a brain injury and enters into a "vegetative state" as a result, might cease to be a person. These are controversial questions that I will not try to address here, but for now it will be helpful to bear in mind that the category of *person* and the category of *human being* are not necessarily identical.
2. A. Cole (n.d.) "Does the Human Body Really Refresh Itself Every Seven Years?" *National Public Radio*. (www.npr.org/sections/health-shots/2016/06/28/483732115/how-old-is-your-body-really).

Introductory Further Readings

Garfield, J., and W. Edelglass (eds.) (2011) *Oxford Handbook of World Philosophy* (New York: Oxford University Press). A volume of essays discussing themes from the world's major philosophical traditions, including contributions on Zen, Korean, and Tibetan Buddhism.

Siderits, M. (2007) *Buddhism as Philosophy* (Indianapolis: Hackett). Luminously clear and informative introduction to central philosophical views in a number of Buddhist traditions.

Advanced Further Readings

Davis, J. (ed.) (2017) *A Mirror Is for Reflecting: Understanding Buddhist Ethics* (New York: Oxford University Press). A collection of recent essays concerned with aspects the ethical stances of various Buddhist traditions.

Ganeri, J. (2015) *The Self: Naturalism, Consciousness, and the First-Person Stance* (Oxford: Oxford University Press). Develops a detailed view of the self inspired by both the classical Indian Buddhist position as well as recent thinking in philosophy in the Western tradition.

Siderits, M., E. Thomson, and D. Zahavi (eds.). (2013) *Self, No-Self: Perspectives From Analytical, Phenomenological, and Indian Traditions* (Oxford: Oxford University Press). State-of-the-art essays on the existence of the self informed by diverse philosophical traditions.

Internet Resources

Velez, A. 'Buddha' in J. Feiser and B. Dowden (eds.) *Internet Encyclopedia of Philosophy* (http://www.iep.utm.edu/buddha/).

Glossary of Terms

ability knowledge: a manifestation of intelligence demonstrating skill. One shows ability knowledge in riding a bicycle or playing an arpeggio on the piano. (Also referred to as "knowledge-how.")

adaptive unconscious: that collection of mental processes that recent experimental psychology has shown to be crucial to our efficient negotiation of the challenges of our environment, both physical and social. Such processes are characterized by automaticity.

affective forecasting: that process by which we make predictions about our future affective state. Experimental psychology has shown human beings to be rather inaccurate in their affective forecasts.

affective state: any emotion or mood, where the former differs from the latter in that they require objects—an answer to what the state is about—while the latter do not. (Shame is an emotion, while anxiety is a mood.)

agnostic: one who is neutral on the question whether God (defined as a being with all possible perfections such as omniscience, omnipotence, omnibenevolence, etc.) exists.

atheist: one who believes that God (defined as a being with all possible perfections such as omniscience, omnipotence, omnibenevolence, etc.) does not exists.

automaticity: that aspect of mental process enabling it to be carried out without our conscious effort. Understanding the meaning of a sentence in a language in which one is fluent will be automatic unless that sentence is ambiguous, very long, or otherwise difficult to process.

category mistake: a mistake in reasoning involving application of a property to an object that could not possibly possess it. (Thinking that the average taxpayer is someone you could meet and shake hands with is a category mistake.) Ryle accuses Descartes of a category mistake in supposing that the mind could exist in an entirely non-physical form.

clear and distinct perception: that epistemological process by which, using the most rigorous and painstaking means at our disposal, we arrive at a conclusion. Descartes uses theological considerations in support of the conclusion that whatever one clearly and distinctly perceives, must also be true.

cognitive state: a mental state involving the processing or storing of information. Beliefs, memories, predictions and conjectures are all cognitive states.

dream interpretation: the process that starts with the manifest content of a dream (what the dreamer experiences) and hypothesizes the latent content of which it is an expression.

dream symbolism: items in dreams that, according to Freud, signify one or more unconscious desire or impulse. (A collection of three objects in a dream, he claims, symbolized male genitalia, for instance.)

dreamwork: the process by which the unconscious mind translates latent content into manifest content.

dualism: an answer to the question, what kind of things exist in the world, stating that at the most basic level there two kinds of things, matter and mind.

epistemology: the study of knowledge, including both ability and propositional knowledge.

experiential state: a mental state or process involving sensory experience (or a process closely related to it such as imagination). Experiencing the taste of lemon, the smell of sulfur, or the touch of velvet at all experiential states or processes.

identity of indiscernibles: if objects x and y have exactly the same properties, then $x = y$. (This doctrine is more controversial than is the indiscernibility of identicals.)

implicit bias: a subconscious state that is a biased attitude toward other groups or individuals based on such factors as skin color, body type, or sexual orientation. A person can harbor only egalitarian attitudes at the conscious level while also harboring implicit biases.

indiscernibility of identicals: If objects x and y are identical, then x and y have exactly the same properties.

infallibility: a conception of self-knowledge associated with Descartes, according to which if one believes that one is in mental state M, then one is in mental state M.

inference to the best explanation: an aspect of scientific method according to which we accept that theory that best accounts for the data available. What counts as "best" in a thoery is characterized by such factors as simplicity, coherence with other established theories, and the theory's posing new question that researchers then go on to answer satisfactorily.

introspection: that process of knowing one's mental states by "looking within."

latent content: the unconscious mental state(s) that become distorted in the production of dreams.

manifest content: that aspect of a dream that the dreamer experiences.

memory link: a psychological relation connecting one person-stage to another. Person-stage P_1 is memory linked to person-stage P_2 just in case P_2 does or can remember an experience had by P_1.

monism: an answer to the question, what kind of things exist in the world, stating that only one kind of thing exists. Monism takes two forms, namely materialistic monism (only material things exist) and idealism (only mental things exist).

parapraxis: Freud's term for what is now called a Freudian slip; a mistake of speaking or some other form of behavior that is caused by an unconscious desire that the agent would have difficulty acknowledging.

persons-stage: a temporal slice of a person who persists through time. Such a stage is likely to have memories, experiences, emotions, and moods.

phosphorescence: a conception of self-knowledge associated with Descartes, according to which if one is in mental state M, then one is also aware of this fact.

primary/secondary qualities: a primary quality is a feature of an object needed to explain its behavior, but which makes no crucial reference to how it affects observers. (Mass and velocity are examples.) A secondary quality is a feature of an object that is needed to explain its impact on normal observers. (Color and smell are examples.)

pre-conscious: unconscious mental states to which we can gain introspective access, although the process of gaining this access may be difficult or even disturbing. Non-conscious states are not necessarily pre-conscious.

propositional knowledge: a psychological state directed toward a proposition. A dominant theme in Western philosophy treats propositional knowledge as requiring (at least) justified, true belief in that proposition. (Also referred to as "knowledge-that.")

reaction-formation: that process by which a subject with an unconscious desire strenuously rejects any stimulation that might activate it.

reduction (eliminative and preservative): We reduce A's to B's by showing that all features characterizing A's can be explained on the hypothesis that A's are really B's. (Lightning is reducible to electrical discharge in this sense). Some reductions are eliminative (enabling us to infer that A's do not exist after all), while others are preservative (enabling us to infer that A's are real, but that positing them does not commit us to anything more than we had already been committed to in positing A's).

self-distancing: that process by which we take a third-personal perspective on ourselves in an effort to respond to emotionally challenging situations.

skepticism: a view in epistemology emphasizing the limitations of our knowledge.

skhanda: a Sanskrit word referring to any collection of like objects.

Socratic method: a dialectical method by which speaker A brings speaker B to a new realization by drawing out from B answers to questions. In the process A does not tell B anything.

somatic marker: a physiologically driven aspect of perceptual experience (including both imagining and memory) causing items of experience to be salient to us in a way relevant to affect. (A pair of gloves owned by someone who has recently died will likely be somatically marked for the grieving survivor.)

subconscious: unconscious mental states to which we cannot gain introspective access. Thus the only way for one to know about one's subconscious mental states is in a third-personal, or extrospective way. Non-conscious states are not necessarily subconscious.

sublimation: the process by which an unconscious desire or impulse is given partial satisfaction by means of a socially acceptable activity. (Sexual desire becomes sublimated in the activity of dancing, for instance.)

theist: one who believes in the existence of God defined as a being with all possible perfections (such as omniscience, omnipotence, omnibenevolence, etc.).

Bibliography

Adams, H., L. Wright, and B. Lohr (1996) 'Is Homophobia Associated With Homosexual Arousal?' *Journal of Abnormal Psychology*, vol. 105, pp. 440–5.

Andrews, K. and J. Beck (eds.). (2017) *Routledge Companion to the Philosophy of Animal Minds* (New York: Routledge).

Andrews, P. (2001) 'The Psychology of Social Chess and the Evolution of Attribution Mechanisms: Explaining the Fundamental Attribution Error,' *Evolution and Human Behavior*, vol. 22, pp. 11–29.

Argue, D., D. Donlon, C. Groves, and R. Wright. (2006) '*Homo Floresiensis*: Microcephalic, Pygmoid, Australopithecus, or Homo?' *Journal of Human Evolution*, vol. 51, pp. 360–74.

Armstrong, D. (1968) *A Materialist Theory of Mind*, Revised Edition (New York: Routledge).

Bargh, J., A. Lee-Chai, K. Barndollar, P. Gollwitzer, and R. Trötschel. (2001) 'The Automated Will: Nonconscious Activation and Pursuit of Behavioral Goals,' *Journal of Personality and Social Psychology*, vol. 81, pp. 1014–27.

Baumeister, R., Dale, K., and K. Sommer (1998) 'Freudian Defense Mechanisms and Empirical Findings in Modern Social Psychology: Reaction Formation, Projection, Displacement, Undoing, Isolation, Sublimation, and Denial,' *Journal of Personality*, vol. 66, pp. 1081–124.

Bertrand, M., D. Chugh, and S. Mullainathan. (2005) 'Implicit Discrimination,' *American Economic Review*, vol. 95, pp. 94–8.

Bowden, H. (2005) *Classical Athens and the Delphic Oracle* (Cambridge: Cambridge University Press).

Brasil-Neto, J. P., A. Pascaul-Leone, J. Valls-Solé, L. G. Cohen, and M. Hallett. (1992) 'Focal Transcranial Magnetic Stimulation and Response Bias in a Forced-choice Task,' *Journal of Neurology, Neurosurgery, and Psychiatry*, vol. 55, pp. 964–6.

Brownstein, M. and J. Saul (eds.). (2016) *Implicit Bias and Philosophy*, Vols. I and II (Oxford: Oxford University Press).

Bushman, B., A. Stack, and R. Baumeister. (1999) 'Catharsis, Aggression, and Persuasive Influence: Self-Fulfilling or Self-Defeating Prophecies?' *Journal of Personality and Social Psychology*, vol. 76, pp. 367–76.

Carmel, D. and M. Sprevak. (2015) 'What Is Consciousness?' in M. Massimi et al. (eds.) *Philosophy and the Sciences for Everyone* (New York: Routledge), pp. 103–22.

Chalmers, D. (2002) *Philosophy of Mind: Classical and Contemporary Readings* (Oxford: Oxford University Press).

Claparède, E. (1911/1951) 'Recognition and "Me-Ness," ' in D. Rapaport (ed.) *Organization and Pathology of Thought* (New York: Columbia University Press), pp. 58–75.

Cole, A. (n.d.) "Does the Human Body Really Refresh Itself Every Seven Years?" National Public Radio. (www.npr.org/sections/health-shots/2016/06/28/483732115/how-old-is-your-body-really).

Coplan, A. and P. Goldie (eds.). (2011) *Empathy: Philosophical and Psychological Perspectives* (Oxford: Oxford University Press).

Cottingham, J. (1992) *The Cambridge Companion to Descartes* (Cambridge: Cambridge University Press).

Crewes, F. (2006) 'The Unknown Freud,' reprinted in his *The Follies of the Wise: Dissenting Essays* (Emeryville, CA: Shoemaker Hoard), pp. 15–42.

Damasio, A. (1994) *Descartes' Error: Emotion, Reason, and the Human Brain* (New York: Penguin).

Davis, J. (ed.) (2017) *A Mirror is for Reflecting: Understanding Buddhist Ethics* (New York: Oxford University Press).

Dawes, R. (1994) *House of Cards: Psychology and Psychotherapy Built on Myth* (New York: Free Press).

Decety, J. (ed.). (2014) *Empathy: From Bench to Bedside* (Cambridge, MA: MIT Press).

Descartes, R. (1993) *Meditations on First Philosophy*, 3rd Edition, ed. D.A. Cress (Indianapolis: Hackett).

Epstein, S. (1994) 'Integration of the Cognitive and Psychodynamic Unconscious,' *American Psychologist*, vol. 49, pp. 709–24.

Fontenrose, J. (1978) *The Delphic Oracle: Its Responses and Operations* (Berkeley: University of California Press).

Freeman, L. (1990) *The Story of Anna O.—The Woman Who Led Freud to Psychoanalysis* (St. Paul, MN: Paragon House).

Ganeri, J. (2015) *The Self: Naturalism, Consciousness, and the First-Person Stance* (Oxford: Oxford University Press).

Gardner, S. (1991) 'The Unconscious,' in J. Neu (ed.) *The Cambridge Companion to Freud* (Cambridge: Cambridge University Press).

Glover, J. (2008) *Choosing Children: Genes, Disability, and Design* (Oxford: Oxford University Press).

Gomez, L. (2005) *The Freud Wars: An Introduction to the Philosophy of Psychoanalysis* (New York and London: Routledge).

Goode, E. (2001) 'Rats May Dream, It Seems, of Their Days at the Mazes,' *New York Times*.

Green, M. (2008) 'Empathy, Expression, and What Artworks Have to Teach,' in G. Hagberg (ed.) *Art and Ethical Criticism* (Oxford: Blackwell), pp. 95–122.

———. (2010) 'How and What Can We Learn From Literature?' in G. Hagberg and W. Jost (eds.) *The Blackwell Companion to the Philosophy of Literature* (Hoboken, NJ: Wiley-Blackwell), pp. 350–66.

———. (2016) 'Learning to Be Good (or Bad) in (or Through) Literature,' in G. Hagberg (ed.) *Fictional Characters, Real Problems: The Search for Ethical Content in Literature* (Oxford: Oxford University Press), pp. 282–304.

Grünbaum, A. (1984) *The Foundations of Psychoanalysis: A Philosophical Critique* (Berkeley: University of California Press).

Halpern, J., and R. Arnold (2008) 'Affective Forecasting: An Unrecognized Challenge in Making Serious Health Decisions,' *Journal of General Internal Medicine*, vol. 23, pp. 1708–1712.

Hatfield, E., J. Cacciopo, and R. Rapson. (1993) *Emotional Contagion* (Cambridge: Cambridge University Press).

Heil, J. (2004) *Philosophy of Mind: A Contemporary Introduction* (New Yorka dn London: Routledge).

Hobbes, T. (1651/1994) *Leviathan, With Selected Variants From the Latin Edition of 1668*, ed. E. Curley (Indianapolis: Hackett).

———. (1655/1981) *Part 1 of De Corpore*, trans. A. P. Martinich (New York: Abaris Books).

Hobson, J. A. (1989) *The Dreaming Brain: How the Brain Creates Both the Sense and Nonsense of Dreams* (New York: Basic Books).

———. (2011) *Dreaming: A Very Short Introduction* (Oxford: Oxford University Press).

Hofmann, W. and T. Wilson. (2010) 'Consciousness, Introspection, and the Adaptive Unconscious,' in B. Gawronski and B. Payne (eds.) *Handbook of Implicit Social Cognition* (New York: Guilford Press), pp. 197–215.

Johnson, P. (2011) *Socrates: A Man for Our Times* (London: Viking).

Kane, R. (2005) *A Contemporary Introduction to Free Will* (New York: Oxford University Press).

Kind, A. (2015) *Persons and Personal Identity* (Malden, MA: Polity Press).

Kitto, H.D.F. (1951) *The Greeks* (London: Penguin).

Kraut, R. (1992) *The Cambridge Companion to Plato* (Cambridge: Cambridge University Press).

———. (2009) 'The Examined Life,' in S. Ahbel-Rapp and R. Kamtakar (eds.) *A Companion to Socrates* (Hoboken, NJ: Wiley-Blackwell), pp. 228–42.

Kross, E., & O. Ayduk (2011) Making Meaning out of Negative Experiences by Self-Distancing,' *Current Directions in Psychological Science*, vol. 20, pp. 187–191.

Kross, E., and I. Grossmann. (2011) 'Boosting Wisdom: Distance from the Self Enhances Wise Reasoning, Attitudes, and Behavior,' *Journal of Experimental Psychology: General*. Vol. 141, pp. 43–48.

La Mettrie, J. (1994) *Man a Machine, and Man a Plant*, trans. R. Watson and M. Rybalka (Indianapolis: Hackett).

Lear, J. (2015) *Freud*, 2nd Edition (London and New York: Routledge).

Levy, N. (2016) 'Implicit Bias and Moral Responsibility: Probing the Data,' *Philosophy and Phenomenological Research*, vol. 94, pp. 3–26.

Libet, B. (1985) 'Unconscious Cerebral Initiative and the Role of Conscious Will in Voluntary Action,' *Behavioral and Brain Sciences*, vol. 8, pp. 529–66.

Lipton, P. (2000) 'Inference to the Best Explanation,' in W. Newton-Smith (ed.) *A Companion to the Philosophy of Science* (Oxford: Blackwell), pp. 184–93.

Locke, J. (1975) *Essay Concerning Human Understanding*, ed. P. Nidditch (Oxford: Oxford University Press).

Lowe, E. J. (2000) *An Introduction to the Philosophy of Mind* (Cambridge: Cambridge University Press).

Lycan, W. (1996) *Consciousness and Experience* (Cambridge, MA: MIT Press).

Macmillan, M. (1991) *Freud Evaluated: The Completed Arc* (North-Holland: Kluwer).

Matheson, J. (2015) 'Disagreement and Epistemic Peers,' in D. Pritchard, ed. *Oxford Handbooks Online* (Oxford: Oxford University Press).

Mele, A. (2009) *Effective Intentions: The Power of Conscious Will* (Oxford: Oxford University Press).

Moffett, M. (2014) *Knowing How: Essays on Knowledge, Mind and Action* (Oxford: Oxford University Press).

Nahmias, E. (2014) 'Is Free Will an Illusion? Confronting Challenges From the Modern Mind Sciences,' in W. Sinnott-Armstrong (ed.) *Moral Psychology, Vol 4: Freedom and Responsibility* (Cambridge, MA: MIT Press), pp. 1–26.

Nails, D. (2009) 'The Trial and Death of Socrates,' in S. Ahbel-Rapp and R. Kamtakar (eds.) *A Companion to Socrates* (Hoboken, NJ: Wiley-Blackwell), pp. 5–20.

Oswald, M. and S. Grosjean (2004) "Confirmation Bias," in R. Pohl (ed.) *Cognitive Illusions: A Handbook of Fallacies and Biases in Thinking, Judgment and Memory* (New York: Psychology Press), pp. 79–96.

Perry, J. (1978) *A Dialogue on Personal Identity and Immortality* (Indianapolis: Hackett).

———. (1978) *Personal Identity* (Berkeley: University of California Press).

———. (2002) *Identity, Personal Identity, and the Self* (Indianapolis: Hackett).

Plato. (2002) *Five Dialogues*, 2nd Edition, trans. G.M.A. Grube and J. M. Cooper (Indianapolis: Hackett).

Pritchard, D. (2009) *Knowledge* (London: Palgrave Macmillan).

———. (2014) 'What Is Knowledge? Do We Have Any?' in M. Chrisman and D. Prichard (eds.) *Philosophy for Everyone* (New York: Routledge), pp. 21–36.

Ravenscroft, I. (2005) *Philosophy of Mind: A Beginner's Guide* (Oxford: Oxford University Press).

Reber, A. (1989) 'Implicit Learning and Tacit Knowledge,' *Journal of Experimental Psychology: General*, vol. 118, pp. 219–35.

Reeve, C. (1989) *Socrates in the Apology: An Essay on Plato's Apology of Socrates* (Indianapolis: Hackett).

Ryle, G. (1949/2009) *The Concept of Mind*, 60th Anniversary Edition, ed. J. Tanney (London and New York: Routledge).

Schechtman, M. (1996) *The Constitution of Selves* (Ithaca, NY: Cornell University Press).

Secada, J. (2013) 'God and Meditation in Descartes' *Meditations on First Philosophy*,' in K. Detlefsen (ed.) *Descartes' Meditations: A Critical Guide* (Cambridge: Cambridge University Press), pp. 200–25.

Siderits, M. (2007) *Buddhism as Philosophy* (Indianapolis, IN: Hackett).

Siderits, M., E. Thomson, and D. Zahavi (eds.). (2013) *Self, No-Self: Perspectives From Analytical, Phenomenological, and Indian Traditions* (Oxford: Oxford University Press).

Sidnell, J. 'Conversation Analysis,' in *Oxford Research Encyclopedia of Linguistics* (http://linguistics.oxfordre.com/view/10.1093/acrefore/9780199384655.001.0001/acrefore-9780199384655-e-40?rskey=IorUad&result=2).

Sorell, T. (2000) *Descartes: A Very Short Introduction* (Oxford: Oxford University Press).

Spiller, H., J. Hale, and J. Z. de Boer. (2003) 'Questioning the Delphic Oracle,' *Scientific American*, vol. 289, pp. 67–73.

Staats, C. (2014) *State of the Science: Implicit Bias Review 2014*, Kirwan Institute, Ohio State University (http://cte.virginia.edu/wp-content/uploads/2016/01/2014-implicit-bias_pp.70-73.pdf).

Sternberg, E. (2010) *My Brain Made Me Do It: The Rise of Neuroscience and the Threat to Moral Responsibility* (Amherst, NY: Prometheus Books).

Stroud, B. (2008) 'Our Debt to Descartes,' in J. Broughton and J. Carriero (eds.) *A Companion to Descartes* (Hoboken, NJ: Wiley-Blackwell).

Taylor, C. (1998) *Socrates: A Very Short Introduction* (Oxford: Oxford University Press).

Wegner, D., and T. Wheatley (1999) 'Apparent Mental Causation: Sources of the Experience of Will,' *American Psychologist*, vol. 54, pp. 80–92.

Weston, D. (1998) 'The Scientific Legacy of Sigmund Freud: Toward a Psychodynamically Informed Psychological Science,' *Psychological Bulletin*, vol. 124, pp. 333–71.

Whitcomb, D., H. Battaly, J. Baehr, and D. Howard-Snyder. (2017) 'Intellectual Humility: Owning Our Limitations,' *Philosophy and Phenomenological Research*, vol. 94, pp. 509–39.

Williams, B. (1978) *Descartes: The Project of Pure Inquiry* (New York: Penguin).

Wilson, M. (1978) *Descartes* (London: Routledge and Kegan Paul).

Wilson, T. (2004) *Strangers to Ourselves: Understanding the Adaptive Unconscious* (Cambridge, MA: Harvard University Press).

———. (2011) *Redirect: Changing the Stories We Live By* (New York: Little, Brown).

Wilson, T. and D. Gilbert. (2005) 'Affective Forecasting: Knowing What to Want,' *Current Directions in Psychological Science*, vol. 14, pp. 131–4.

Zemack-Rugar, Y., J. Bettman, and G. Fitzsimons. (2007) 'The Effects of Non-Consciously Priming Emotion Concepts on Behavior,' *Journal of Personality and Social Psychology*, vol. 93, pp. 927–39.

Index

Made in the USA
Monee, IL
10 October 2022

15580794R00089